Sustainability

Short Introductions series

Sustainability

Maurie J. Cohen

polity

Polity Press
65 Bridge Street
Cambridge CB2 1UR, UK

Polity Press
101 Station Landing
Suite 300
Medford, MA 02155, USA

ISBN-13: 978-1-5095-4031-0
ISBN-13: 978-1-5095-4032-7 (pb)

A catalogue record for this book is available from the British Library.

Library of Congress Cataloging-in-Publication Data
Names: Cohen, Maurie J, author.
Title: Sustainability / Maurie J Cohen.
Description: Medford : Polity Press, 2020. | Series: Short introductions | Includes bibliographical references and index. | Summary: "Authoritative introduction to one of the most important challenges of the 21st century"-- Provided by publisher.
Identifiers: LCCN 2020015885 (print) | LCCN 2020015886 (ebook) | ISBN 9781509540310 (hardback) | ISBN 9781509540327 (paperback) | ISBN 9781509540334 (epub)
Subjects: LCSH: Sustainable development. | Environmental engineering. | Social change.
Classification: LCC HC79.E5 C595 2020 (print) | LCC HC79.E5 (ebook) | DDC 304.2--dc23
LC record available at https://lccn.loc.gov/2020015885
LC ebook record available at https://lccn.loc.gov/2020015886

Typeset in 10 on 12pt Sabon
by Fakenham Prepress Solutions, Fakenham, Norfolk NR21 8NL
Printed and bound in Great Britain by CPI Group (UK) Ltd, Croydon

For further information on Polity, visit our website: politybooks.com

Contents

Figures, Tables, and Boxes

Acknowledgments

While the writing of this book was compressed into a few months, the final product is more accurately understood as an outcome of nearly three decades of work and reflection. I originally became interested in many of the themes discussed in this volume during the years following the Earth Summit held in Rio de Janeiro in 1992. My interest was initially perked while in my first academic position in the United States, at the School of Public and Environmental Affairs at Indiana University and then, in the United Kingdom, as the Ove Arup Research Fellow at the Centre for Environment, Ethics, and Society (OCEES) at Mansfield College, University of Oxford.

The mid- and late 1990s marked an especially fertile era for nascent sustainability-focused activities in the United Kingdom. The intellectual firmament was in flux and new space was opening up for innovative areas of inquiry. It was also a time when, across large parts of Europe, there was a high level of public interest and political engagement on associated issues. This attentiveness propelled research and practice and led to the development of the field of sustainability social science that informs significant parts of this book. I am grateful to my colleagues at OCEES at the time, including Avner de Shalit, Graham Dutfield, Antonia Layard, Joseph Murphy, Jouni Paavola, Neil Summerton, Bhaskar Vira, and the late Darrell Posey.

Upon returning to the United States at the start of the new millennium, it was revealing to discover that in American higher education the sustainability arc had not yet begun to bend in the same direction. After two years teaching environmental policy and politics at Binghamton University (State University of New York), I joined the Environmental

Policy Studies Program at the New Jersey Institute of Technology (NJIT), where most of my students were simultaneously pursuing a graduate degree and working as staff members of the state's Department of Environmental Protection. Sustainability was not exactly on the tip of everyone's tongue, but I was heartened that it was not an entirely foreign concept. Many of the issues discussed in this book began to take pedagogical shape in courses that I delivered during those years.

Since 2012, I have been the coordinator of the Program in Science, Technology, and Society at NJIT, and in this administrative role instigated the establishment of a curricular option that enables students from various disciplines to conjoin their primary degree with a secondary specialization in sustainability studies. Given the university's focus on applied science, engineering, and the design arts, aspiring architects and designers have disproportionately filled the ranks, though in recent years I have welcomed growing numbers of undergraduates from engineering departments. I regard this experience as evidence that a broadening range of students is becoming cognizant of the need to take prompt action to ensure a more sustainable future for both people and planet.

This book also owes its existence to my activities with the Future Earth Knowledge-Action Network on Systems of Sustainable Consumption and Production (KAN SSCP). Special thanks go to the Research Institute for Humanity and Nature in Kyoto for generously hosting this group. I am appreciative of extremely productive collaboration with Magnus Bengtsson, Charlotte Jensen, Ria Lambino, Sylvia Lorek, Hein Mallee, Steven McGreevy, Masami Oka, and Patrick Schröder.

I also owe a debt of gratitude to my partners from various related and other projects over the past few years and take this opportunity to acknowledge Joseph Blasi, Anna Davies, Leonie Dendler, Paul Dewick, Karin Ekström, Amy Forrester, David Hess, Melanie Jaeger-Erben, Emily Huddart Kennedy, Naomi Krogman, Oksana Mont, Maisam Najafizada, Eilise Norris, Jaco Quist, Lucia Reisch, Thomas Reuter, Marlyne Sahakian, Joseph Sarkis, Dimitris Stevis, Arnold Tukker, Daniel Welch, and Esthi Zipori.

My heartfelt thanks to Louise Knight at Polity for inviting me to contribute to the Short Introductions series and to Inès Boxman for ensuring that I did not deviate from a strict timetable for bringing the manuscript to completion. Evie Deavall and Sarah Dancy expertly assisted in getting the book across the finish line and Leigh Priest prepared the index.

My three children, Lydia, Alexander, and Jeremy, eagerly and enthusiastically accompanied me on many of the excursions that inform this volume. My wife, Patricia, is a shrewd critic who never wavers in telling me when I have rushed to a conclusion or generalized from insufficient evidence. It is to my family that I lovingly dedicate this book.

Abbreviations

ANS	Adjusted Net Savings
APF	Alaska Permanent Fund
BREEAM	Building Research Establishment Environmental Assessment Method
CBD	Convention on Biological Diversity
CSD	Commission on Sustainable Development
EFA	Ecological Footprint Analysis
EMS	Environmental Management System
ESEM	Earth System Engineering and Management
FDI	Foreign Direct Investment
GCM	global Citizens Movement
GDP	Gross Domestic Product
GEF	Global Environmental Facility
GFN	Global Footprint Network
GND	Green New Deal
GNH	Gross National Happiness
GPGP	Great Pacific Garbage Patch
GPI	Genuine Progress Indicator
GSSA	Global Standard Stratigraphic Age
GSSP	Global Boundary Stratotype Section and Point
GTI	Great Transition Initiative
GTS	Geologic Time Scale
HDI	Human Development Index
HPI	Happy Planet Index
ICS	International Commission on Stratigraphy
ICT	Information and Communication Technologies

IGBP	International Geosphere-Biosphere Programme
IMF	International Monetary Fund
IPCC	Intergovernmental Panel on Climate Change
ISEW	Index of Sustainable Economic Welfare
IUCN	International Union for the Conservation of Nature
IUGS	International Union of Geological Sciences
JPI	Johannesburg Plan of Implementation
LCA	Life Cycle Analysis
LEED	Leadership in Energy and Environmental Design
LETS	Local Exchange Trading System
LPI	Living Planet Index
MDG	Millennium Development Goals
MIT	Massachusetts Institute of Technology
MLP	Multi-Level Perspective
MT/P	Metric Tons Per Person
NASA	National Aeronautics and Space Administration
NDP	Net Domestic Product
NEF	New Economics Foundation
NGO	Nongovernmental Organization
ODA	Overseas Development Assistance
OECD	Organisation for Economic Co-operation and Development
PPM	Parts Per Million
RMI	Rocky Mountain Institute
SDG	Sustainable Development Goals
STEM	Science, Technology, Engineering, and Math
TEP	Techno-Economic Paradigm
TMC	Total Material Consumption
TNSP	The Next System Project
TRI	Toxic Release Inventory
UBI	Universal Basic Income
UNCCD	United Nations Convention to Combat Desertification
UNCED	United Nations Conference on Environment and Development (Rio de Janeiro 1992)
UNCHE	United Nations Conference on the Human Environment (Stockholm 1972)
UNCSD	United Nations Conference on Sustainable Development (Rio de Janeiro 2012)
UNDP	United Nations Development Programme
UNEP	United Nations Environment Programme
UNESCO	United Nations Educational, Scientific, and Cultural Organization
UNFCCC	United Nations Framework Convention on Climate Change

UNHLPFSD	United Nations High-Level Political Forum on Sustainable Development
USCSD	United Nations Conference on Sustainable Development
WCED	World Commission on Environment and Development
WGA	Working Group on the Anthropocene
WSSD	World Summit on Sustainable Development (Johannesburg 2002)

1

What Is Sustainability?

Introduction

Imagine this situation. You come home after a long day. You turn on the television news and the first story concerns a "king tide flood" in Florida. You have never heard this term, so you turn up the volume and listen intently as the reporter describes scenes of rivulets bubbling up from storm sewers, waves lapping over the top of seawalls, and water puddling up in coastal roads. The local government has invested more than $100 million in recent years to install pumping stations and a complex network of pipes to reduce the severity of the problem, which is due to the rising level of the Atlantic Ocean. Despite the assurances of hydrological engineers, this new equipment has done little to reduce the flooding, which is particularly severe in the spring when incoming tides are at their annual highs. The story ends with a grim commentary. This is just the early stage and the inundations will become worse with each passing year. Because of the ongoing accumulation of carbon dioxide and other greenhouse gases in the atmosphere, average global temperatures are on track to exceed the 1.5°C threshold that climate scientists contend will lead to catastrophic impacts. Sea levels will continue to rise and forecasts indicate that as much as one third of the state's landmass will end up submerged by 2100.

After a brief commercial break, the next report is about a small village in the Canadian province of Nova Scotia. The images on the screen show charming clapboard houses and, in the distance, red cliffs with beaches bordered by sand dunes. Thirty years ago, captains of local fishing boats caught as much cod as they could fit into their storage holds. But no longer. The fishery collapsed along with the optimism of residents who relied on this seemingly inexhaustible resource for their livelihoods. After graduating from high school these days, most young people see little reason to stay in town and instead move to Halifax or Toronto where there are much more lucrative and dependable job opportunities. The remaining population is getting older and struggling to make ends meet. Local stores are closing and there is talk that it is just a matter of time before the regional educational authority decides to close down the local schools. A rumor has started to circulate that the hospital is facing serious financial hardship.

A third story shows hundreds of people standing next to a flatbed truck while two men in uniform pass out cartons of bottled water. As the camera pans around, it becomes apparent that this is not a wealthy community. The houses are modest and in need of repair, and looking further down the street it is possible to discern the faint outlines of shuttered factories and empty parking lots. Scattered about are rusting metal signs warning residents to stay away from these vast open spaces because of toxic chemicals that were long ago buried under the pavement. The reporter explains that, earlier in the day, the mayor declared that the local water supply was not safe to drink. Tests had revealed that lead was leaching from the aging pipes. It would be months – perhaps years – before the problem would be resolved. In the meantime, local officials would distribute boxes of water three times each week.

You push back onto the sofa and wonder what these three dismaying depictions – a municipality inundated by coastal flooding, a village in distress because of a collapsed fishery, and a former industrial city suffering from lead poisoning – have in common. Different though they are, all are examples of what can go wrong when we disregard the essential interactions that occur between people and the surrounding environment. They also offer instructive evidence of how problems that may initially seem to be the result of scientific or technological mishaps are, after closer inspection, more correctly attributable to a wider range of factors.

It is getting late and a final report of the night begins to roll as you start to fall asleep. The scene has an air of familiarity. You stir yourself back into wakefulness, but are not sure whether the images remind you of a place you visited some years ago, or perhaps read about in a book. Or maybe someone just told you about it in a mostly forgotten conversation. The people on the screen appear to be relatively prosperous, but not in the ordinary way. Families reside in well-kempt houses, though you notice that the dwellings are somewhat smaller than is commonplace today in most rich countries. Additionally, each home is outfitted with a solar array for generating energy for the household. Throughout the neighborhood, there are easily accessible recreation centers, communal kitchens, and medical facilities. Residents get around town on bicycles, scooters, and other personal mobility devices. The only vehicles in view are for emergency services, deliveries, and some municipal operations – and these are all electric powered. There is a convivial spirit throughout the community and people are engaged in a diverse and elaborate assortment of daily activities that include formal employment, volunteer service, artistry, and childcare and eldercare. The final segment of the program shows a handwritten placard on the front door of a house that says, "Sustainability, It's a Lifestyle!"

It is apparent that this community offers a stark contrast to the three reports featured in the earlier part of the newscast. You think about the various places you have lived over the years, but none is particularly memorable. The recollection that comes most readily to mind is spending so much time driving back and forth along the same monotonous stretches of highway, often squandering hours stuck in mind-numbing traffic. You begin to grow hungry and think that it would be great to be able to have your own backyard garden like the people you just saw on television. Perhaps you will give that idea more thought tomorrow. Deep down, though, you know that it is unlikely to happen because you need to work so many hours and when you get home you are so exhausted. But what did that evocative sign about sustainability and lifestyle mean?

How Did We Get Here?

Sustainability is oftentimes interpreted as a kind of supercharged version of environmentalism – a set of practices undertaken by people who are a tad more serious about, for instance, eating less meat, saving some energy, or purchasing "greener" products. It is important to note at the onset that these preferences are not without merit, but this book adopts a more expansive conception. Our perspective contends that sustainability is not only about expedient adjustments in individual behavior. The objective is to demonstrate that a more environmentally tenable and socially equitable future is predicated on a range of innovations. We need to spark a transition in how we conduct science, practice engineering, and, perhaps most importantly, organize society.

Vast systems exist for mining and harvesting natural resources, for assembling raw materials into fabricated materials, for manufacturing components into industrial products, and for discarding finished goods when they have ceased to have discernible value. Along the way, and sometimes counterpoised with periods of relative prosperity, these activities impose adverse consequences in the form of industrial pollution, natural resource depletion, and social upheaval. For a long time, we mostly overlooked these effects. They were ignored because of a perception that the financial returns were larger than the costs of the inflicted damages or because the victims did not have sufficient political power to protect themselves.

Concern for the environmental security of the planet and the livelihoods of its most vulnerable and disempowered inhabitants has tended to evolve episodically and in tandem with other processes of social change. Disruptions during the nineteenth century prompted by the intertwined processes of industrialization and urbanization gave rise to new sensibilities about the availability of vital natural resources and mobilized efforts to rectify the dangerously unhealthy conditions that persisted at the time in densely populated cities. The most critical issues, as well as strategies for improvement, varied from one place to another and were both enabled and constrained by prevailing social norms, economic circumstances, and political opportunities. For instance, the River Thames in London previously served as a cesspool for the dumping of human bodily wastes, offal from butchered animals, and industrial effluents. During the summer of 1858, the stench became so odious that it prompted construction of one of the first sewage treatment plants and the passage of new laws to limit discharges (Halliday 2001).

In North America, explorers, surveyors, and adventurers returned home during the early decades of the nineteenth century with astonishing reports of transcendent landscapes, abounding wildlife, and fearsome indigenous tribes. At the same time, population dispersal and agricultural expansion were, with each passing year, pushing the frontier further westward and prompting prophetic observers to speculate whether unchecked settlement would deny future generations the opportunity to experience the wondrous natural treasures. Others were inspired to action out of a sense of unease that rapacious exploitation would destroy the regenerative potential of forests, fisheries, and other renewable resources. Such concerns gradually led to the implementation of scientific management to control the most devastating practices and to ensure the ongoing availability of these living engines of prosperity (Worster 1993).

During the post-World War II era, these earlier measures proved insufficient to stem the rising tide of industrial pollution and the voracious appetite of producers for raw materials. Initially, a rising tide of wealth diverted attention from the deteriorating environmental conditions unfolding in affluent countries. However, by the 1960s growing numbers of people were no longer inclined to disregard the flagrant and persistent abuses accumulating in both urban and rural areas. The two aforementioned currents – urban public health and responsible use of natural resources – fused together into an increasingly coherent and formidable social movement intent on pressuring the political system to implement environmental reforms (Gottlieb 1993).

The late nineteenth and early twentieth centuries also marked a period of expanding influence for labor unions, antipoverty associations, and social welfare advocates across large parts of Europe, North America, and Australasia. Responding to the pronounced patterns of inequality that characterized industrial society at the time, these organizations sought to give greater social and political visibility to the poor. Their efforts took the form of campaigns to improve housing conditions, to reduce working hours, to provide cash allowances and other forms of social protection, to expand access to education, and to establish progressive systems of taxation. While overall commitment and effectiveness varied across countries, ameliorating the conditions of extreme poverty came to be regarded as a societal undertaking with particular responsibility assigned to government.

During the immediate aftermath of World War II, the United Nations adopted the Universal Declaration of Human Rights in 1948, which affirms "the equal and inalienable rights of all members of the human family." It states in Article 22 that everyone "has the right to social security and is entitled to realization, through national effort and international co-operation and in accordance with the organization and resources of each State, of the economic, social and cultural rights indispensable for his dignity and the free development of his personality." Article 25 further asserts: "Everyone has the right to a standard of living adequate for the health and well-being of himself and of his family, including food, clothing, housing and medical care and necessary social services." These commitments are today regarded as "customary international law" and most countries have incorporated them into their constitutions and other national framework legislation. In subsequent years, nations around the world have endorsed a number of other covenants intended to focus attention on poverty reduction, including the Convention on the Elimination of All Forms of Racial Discrimination (1969), the Convention on the Elimination of All Forms of Discrimination Against Women (1979), and the Convention on the Rights of the Child (1989).

In the international sphere, mounting concern about poverty and its connections to the natural environment became a matter of special concern during the dissolution of formalized colonialism during the 1950s and 1960s. Beginning with India in 1948, large parts of Africa and Asia that had previously been imperial dependencies governed by foreign powers secured independence. The process of disengagement was in many cases fraught with conflict and violence. The challenges of nation-building were magnified by the pronounced political tensions between, on the one hand, the United States and its allies and, on the other, the Soviet Union and its satellite states. Fragile, newborn countries frequently found themselves having to choose sides in this ideological and military rivalry and these entanglements drained resources from efforts to overcome colonial legacies. Problems were further compounded by the need to participate in systems of international trade and finance that were massively disadvantageous and locked emergent nations into dependent relationships. The period also brought into view the interconnections between entrenched economic inequality, endemic poverty, unfair appropriation of natural resource wealth, and environmental degradation.

The global system came to be divided into three domains: the "first world" comprised the United States and "the rest of the West," the "second world" included the Soviet Union and other countries in its sphere of influence, and the "third world" encompassed primarily the former colonial dependencies (most of which were located in the southern hemisphere). The first and second worlds had variously progressed through intensive processes of industrialization during the nineteenth and twentieth centuries, developed into increasingly urbanized societies, accumulated significant amounts of wealth (despite the destruction imposed by two world wars), and, broadly speaking, attained relatively high material standards of living. By contrast, third world countries had only weakly and incompletely industrialized (or did not experience industrialization at all), remained largely rural and reliant on either subsistence agriculture or economically unfavorable forms of primary production, and had substantially lower levels of per capita income.

Beginning in the 1960s, numerous initiatives were launched to narrow this chasm. First, national governments established agencies to provide funding for overseas development assistance (ODA), to create educational exchange programs, and to facilitate technology transfer.[1] Second, multilateral institutions – most notably the World Bank and the International Monetary Fund (IMF) – offered financing to lower-income countries for infrastructure projects and to buffer hardship due to economic crises. Third, transnational corporations were encouraged to locate production facilities and other operations in the less developed nations through processes of foreign direct investment (FDI). Finally, building on practices instituted during the nineteenth century by religious groups and medical associations, numerous nongovernmental organizations (NGOs) became engaged in providing a patchwork of relief and developmental services.[2]

It was out of this context that the issue of sustainable development (or sustainability as it would come to be recast) began to coalesce. During the 1970s, it became increasingly apparent that financial assistance directed to developing countries frequently failed to achieve its intended objectives because projects perversely exacerbated patterns of environmental degradation such as desertification, deforestation, and soil erosion. Rarely did donor countries and NGOs assess the consequences that their activities might have on ecological conditions. It took time, but eventually awareness began to build that if resource-conservation strategies were to improve livelihoods in poorer countries, it would be necessary to conduct integrated and comprehensive assessments of the possible impacts of economic policies on natural systems.

Recognition of the connections between development and the environment – or "ecodevelopment" as it was termed at the time – crystalized in 1980 with publication of the *World Conservation Strategy* by the International Union for the Conservation of Nature (IUCN 1980).[3] The report affirmed that the aim should be to enhance compatibility between development and conservation and to recognize that economic growth could contribute to effective environmental management. The authors acknowledged that building up the necessary governance capacity to achieve this goal at both national and global scales – especially with respect to scientific knowledge, planning procedures, legal frameworks, personnel, and financial tools – would require very substantial investments. Furthermore, any effort to roll back the entrenched emphasis on industrially driven expansion or re-envision alternative developmental pathways would confront powerful opposition from numerous quarters. Finally, as noted by political scientist John McCormick (1986: 186), for all its emphasis on forging a new paradigm, the *World Conservation Strategy* "limit[ed] itself to the conservation of nature and natural resources ... and paid little heed to the fact that the problems faced by the natural environment are part of the broader issues related to the human environment. The two cannot be divorced."

Also significant at the time was the work of the Independent Commission on International Development Issues chaired by Willy Brandt, former Chancellor of the Federal Republic of Germany. Initially set up in response to a proposition by the World Bank, the so-called Brandt Commission included representatives from both developed and developing countries and pursued its work in a spirit of mutual interest. The intent was not to produce a technical report but rather to influence public opinion, to seek new ideas regarding the design of successful development programs, and to foster recognition of interdependence among a diverse array of countries.

The Commission produced two reports, *North–South: A Program for Survival* (ICIDI 1980) and *Common Crisis North–South: Cooperation for World Recovery* (Brandt Commission 1983), and formalized the distinction between the rich (first world) countries of the global North and poorer nations of the global South. While the demarcation – what came to be known as the Brandt Line – runs roughly along the 30° North latitude, it deviates conspicuously to include Australia and New Zealand (see Figure 1.1). Though the legitimacy of this partition has become increasingly disputed (Navarro 1984; Solarz 2012), the work of the Commission remains notable for elevating environmental and humanitarian issues and linking them to customary matters of international affairs such as monetary policy, financial regulation, and global security.

A second investigatory panel, the Independent Commission on Disarmament and Security Issues led by former Swedish Prime Minister Olof Palme, was launched at roughly the same time. The Commission published its final report entitled *Common Security* in 1982, which was a particularly volatile phase in the Cold War between the United States and the Soviet Union (ICDSI 1982). The document argued that effective security required collective action and that over the long run no single country could act on its own narrowly circumscribed military interests. Security must be constructed by coordinating with adversaries or, as stated in the report, "States can no longer seek security at each other's expense; it can be obtained only through cooperative undertakings."

Most popular attention devoted to the work of the Palme Commission centered on its recommendation to create a "battlefield nuclear-weapon free zone" in Europe. However, the element of the document that is most immediately relevant is its discussion about the counterproductive expenditure of scarce resources by developing countries on military weaponry. These arms purchases depleted national budgets and diverted money that could otherwise be invested in social programs, education, and other initiatives to overcome poverty. Preoccupation with military preparedness was further problematic because it pulled developing countries into Great Power battles where they became pawns in proxy fights, did little to advance their own national interests, and undermined rather than enhanced security. Moreover, the continual threat of conflict amplified the challenges of improving well-being, human rights, social justice, and environmental quality.

While we can trace the emergence of sustainability as a focal objective for a more socially and environmentally secure future back to the conceptual advances contained in these three international commissions, this is only part of the story. The evolution of these priorities from the margins of international affairs to a central focus for policymaking across a large expanse of contemporary society – national governments, municipal agencies, corporations, community organizations, universities, and more – is also attributable to broader currents of social change.

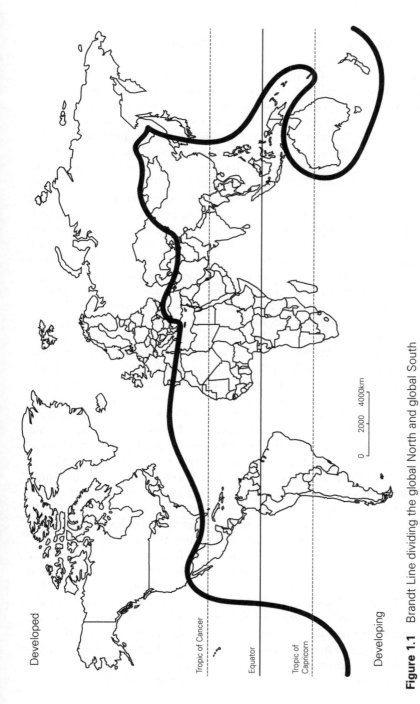

Figure 1.1 Brandt Line dividing the global North and global South

Source: ©User:Jovan.gec / Wikimedia Commons / CC-BY-SA-4.0: https://creativecommons.org/licenses/by-sa/4.0/deed.en.

Sustainability in the Popular Imagination

During the mid-1960s, the fabled innovator and social entrepreneur, Stewart Brand, displayed a stickpin button that posed the question, "Why haven't we seen a photograph of the whole Earth yet?" Even in the psychedelic social scene of San Francisco at the time, this was a curious inquiry. Notwithstanding, a few days prior to Christmas in 1968, three astronauts blasted off in a Saturn rocket from the Kennedy Space Center in Florida and later beamed back home the image that Brand had been yearning to see (Cosgrove 1994; Turner 2008). Evocatively titled *Earthrise*, the picture captured a gibbous and illuminated planet against the inky blackness of the infinite cosmos. The poet Archibald MacLeish, writing on the front page of the *New York Times*, observed: "To see the earth as it truly is, small and blue and beautiful in that eternal silence where it floats, is to see ourselves as riders on the earth together." Four years later, a second, but ultimately more celebrated and iconic, image, *Whole Earth*, crisply depicted the planet with billowy clouds, readily recognizable landmasses, and oceanic expanses. This photograph soon became the most popular picture of all time, emblazoned on everything from tee shirts to coffee cups (Poole 2008).

The ubiquity, to say nothing of the commercial success, of these depictions diverted attention from the more significant achievement, namely that they ushered in a new age of human consciousness, spiritual cognizance, and planetary awareness. Despite no shortage of prior ingenious schemes – from hot-air balloons outfitted with photographic equipment to camera-toting kites – it had not previously been possible to apprehend the entire expanse of the Earth. Due to the extraordinary technological prowess of the National Aeronautics and Space Administration (NASA) and the skillfulness of its astronauts, it was no longer possible to ignore the irrefutable fact that all humanity, as well as other living beings, were united in biospheric citizenship.

This new cosmological conception triggered an onslaught of survivalist-oriented metaphors designed to capture the *zeitgeist* of the era. For instance, some imaginative scientists characterized the planet as a "spaceship" and others asserted that earthly beings needed to band together in "lifeboats" to ensure their security (Boulding 1966; Fuller 1970; Hardin 1974; see also Larson 2014).[4] New environmental organizations mobilized and spurred the establishment of insurgent social movements to press governments and transnational bodies to implement measures to mitigate the most acute ecological abuses. At the international level, prominent groups were Greenpeace and Friends of the Earth, but also influential was a host of more specialized and targeted initiatives focused on the protection of endangered ecosystems, wildlife conservation, and marine environments (Weyler 2004; Thompson 2017).

A string of notorious disasters, including the methylmercury poisoning of Minamata Bay in Japan, the toxic contamination of the Love Canal community in New York State, the Bhopal chemical tragedy in India, the nuclear accidents at Three Mile Island in the United States and Chernobyl in Ukraine, and the occurrence of several catastrophic oil spills, galvanized public attention. A general impression emerged that, during the years following World War II, industrialized (and industrializing) countries had made some ill-fated decisions as part of their headlong pursuit of economic growth.

From the standpoint of today, and acknowledging that the human story does not always unfold in a straight line, it is clear that the remarkable achievements of a half-century ago had a profound effect. New and persistent questions took hold about the efficacy of technological progress, the utility of contemporary measures of prosperity, and the need to align societal ambitions with the resilience of the natural environment. We have further learned over the ensuing decades that customary systems for provisioning human needs – agriculture, industrial production, energy, and transportation – can actively undermine individual and societal well-being. For instance, a clear-eyed visit to a local supermarket in the United States, regardless of the number of organic vegetables on display, is a testament to the fact that the prevailing food system fails the most basic tests of environmental and social responsibility. At the global scale, despite extraordinary achievements in China and other once-poor countries over the past few decades to lift millions of households from deprivation, more than a third of the world's nearly 8 billion people continue to suffer from extreme poverty. Making the problem even more urgent is that human numbers are on track to increase to an estimated 10 billion by 2050 and most of this demographic increase will occur in the world's most impoverished countries.[5]

Sustainability Takes Root

The global circulation of NASA's photographs of the Earth from space triggered an unprecedented wave of political activism, scientific research, and legislation. Environmentalists in dozens of countries around the world mobilized masses of people to participate in public demonstrations on the first Earth Day on April 22, 1970. An estimated 20 million campaigners turned out in the United States for this inaugural event and the scale expanded globally over the following years. By 1990, an estimated 200 million people in more than 140 countries were commemorating Earth Day (Christofferson 2004; Rome 2014).

Soon after the maiden observance of Earth Day, a group of computer scientists based at the Massachusetts Institute of Technology (MIT) published *Limits to Growth*, a shattering report that relied on modeling simulations to explore the relationships between resource availability, industrial output, demographic growth, food production, and environmental quality (Meadows et al. 1972). The upshot of the study was that ceaseless increases in manufacturing production and global population would outstrip resource supplies and cause protracted ecological degradation, ultimately creating conditions for societal collapse. The book sold 30 million copies and was translated into 30 different languages. Critics nonetheless loudly denounced its methodology and conclusions, castigating the authors as irresponsible catastrophists who were recklessly putting human prosperity at severe risk.

In this same timeframe, the United Nations, the Swedish government, and an international network of NGOs convened the United Nations Conference on the Human Environment (UNCHE). In large part the brainchild of Canadian diplomat Maurice Strong, the gathering brought to Stockholm thousands of government officials, activists, scientists, and observers for two weeks of strategizing, protesting, and celebrating under the theme of "Only One Earth." The luminary of the conference was the Prime Minister of India, Indira Gandhi, who delivered the keynote address and sought from the start to overturn complacency. She challenged the assembled group and admonished other world leaders who had stayed away, remonstrating, "Are not poverty and need the greatest polluters? ... It would be ironic if the fight against pollution were to be converted into another business, out of which a few companies, corporations or nations would make profits at the cost of the many." These sentiments would in due course come to inform the emergent concept of sustainable development in powerful ways. Other notable accomplishments included the creation of the United Nations Environment Programme (UNEP), which emerged during the 1970s as the primary institution of global environmental governance.

In 1973, the Yom Kippur (Arab–Israeli) War prompted major oil-producing countries to impose an embargo on the export of oil to countries deemed friendly to Israel. This action resulted in the retail price of gasoline increasing by upwards of 400 percent and setting off alarm bells around the world about energy security. The circumstances tapped into a number of escalating anxieties centered on petroleum dependency and energy inefficiency and led to new interest in renewable sources and less energy-reliant lifestyles (Jacobs 2016). Both presaging and amplifying this interest was publication of economist E. F. Schumacher's *Small*

Is Beautiful (1973) and physicist Amory Lovins's *Soft Energy Paths* (1977). The two volumes, in their own ways, catalyzed different ways of thinking about sustainability, the former encouraging the downsizing of scale and the adoption of less material-intensive livelihoods and the latter sparking a focus on ecologically informed technological innovation.

From the standpoint of geopolitics, the 1970s was, however, a treacherous decade characterized by protracted and dangerous confrontation between the United States and the Soviet Union. In fact, Moscow had refused to send a delegation to the Stockholm conference and the ongoing standoff between the two nuclear powers limited opportunities for multilateral progress in international affairs. Nonetheless, communities of scientists, NGO and civil society representatives, and mid-level government officials continued to meet and to incubate the nascent concept of sustainable development.

The 1979 Iranian Revolution triggered a second oil crisis, more than doubling gasoline prices and resurrecting experiences of just a few years earlier. Popular anxiety again took hold, with long lines at filling stations and widespread apprehension about energy insecurity and fossil-fuel scarcity. The pervasive sense of unease had palpable political ramifications, especially in the United States. President Carter installed solar panels and a wood-burning stove in the White House and gave a televised speech on July 15, in which he famously intoned that:

> In a nation that was proud of hard work, strong families, close-knit communities, and our faith in God, too many of us now tend to worship self-indulgence and consumption. Human identity is no longer defined by what one does, but by what one owns. But we've discovered that owning things and consuming things does not satisfy our longing for meaning. We've learned that piling up material goods cannot fill the emptiness of lives which have no confidence or purpose.[6]

This message of sufficiency resonated with certain parts of the American public, but the vast majority of the country was not persuaded to embrace the material sacrifices implied by the commentary. Carter was decisively defeated in the 1980 presidential election by Ronald Reagan, who offered a far sunnier prognosis. A year earlier, Reagan's ideological partner, Margaret Thatcher, had become Prime Minster of the United Kingdom and the two leaders worked in concert to overturn the political orthodoxy of the post-World War II era, not only in their own nations but far beyond as well. The duo ushered in a decades-long period where social democracy gave way in much of the world to neoliberal priorities predicated on the withdrawal of public financing for social services, the sale of government-owned companies to private interests, and the rollback of environmental and other regulations.

This retreat flew in the face of – and at least for a time further empowered – the national and international movements for environmental protection and social justice that, during the prior decade, had achieved significant institutional stature. A major opportunity emerged in 1983 when the United Nations Secretary-General Javier Pérez de Cuéllar appointed Gro Harlem Brundtland, a former Norwegian Prime Minister, to convene the World Commission on Environment and Development (WCED).[7] Members embarked on a multiyear process of fact-finding, data-gathering, and public meetings, ultimately publishing their final report in 1987 under the title *Our Common Future*. The document is noteworthy today for having established sustainable development as a core objective of development policy planning and seeking to reconcile the tensions between safeguarding the environment and fostering economic growth. It is also important for introducing what is still today the most prevalent definition of sustainable development: "Sustainable development is development that meets the needs of the present without compromising the ability of future generations to meet their own needs."

While numerous sustainability experts have embraced this understanding, it has simultaneously attracted considerable critical attention and it is useful to highlight three of these points (Mitcham 1995; Borowy 2014). First, the Brundtland definition tacitly presumes that there is universal agreement on the specific features and general efficacy of (Western conceptions) of development. Moreover, given ordinary understanding of "development" as a linear process of advancement, how can we envisage the progression to be "sustainable"? Second, the formulation speaks about "needs" in the generic sense without making any distinction between basic needs with respect to food, clothing, and shelter and other requirements that transcend fundamental conditions for survival. Third, the definition contains an awkward conceit, namely that we in the present are realistically able to anticipate the requirements of future generations. Finally, the conventional definition is – and this is the most critical omission in the minds of many critical observers – completely silent on whether humanity faces biophysical limits on economic growth.

It would be naive to presume that the Brundtland Commission was unaware of the ambiguity inherent in how it formalized the concept. The members were working in a politically divisive context and found themselves needing to balance a variety of competing perspectives: business vs. civil society, urban vs. rural, high-income countries vs. low-income countries, and global North vs. global South. They sought to devise a definition that, while perhaps murky, would not be fundamentally objectionable to any of these constituencies. As a result, the

Commission purposefully advanced a conception that it knew from the start was a bit woolly.[8]

However, in situations where it is necessary to ensure broad appeal, fuzziness and imprecision can be strategically advantageous. In fact, political scientists have long been aware of the constructive role that equivocal language plays in policy dialogues; they refer to such expressions as "essentially contested concepts." Furthermore, there is no shortage of this kind of terminology in contemporary political discourse, with familiar examples including "freedom," "liberty," and "democracy." The beneficial value of such concepts is that their vagueness allows people to come together and seek common purpose. This does not mean to suggest that eventual agreement on more substantive issues will come easily, but without some implicit compromises at the outset, it is unlikely that a conversation could even begin. Accordingly, we can regard sustainability as a large table around which the holders of divergent perspectives can gather.

The Brundtland Commission also recognized that it would be necessary to ensure continued commitment on the part of international institutions, governments, and civil society. To achieve this objective, the report proposed holding a global conference on a regularly scheduled basis to compel national representatives to report on their achievements. Such gatherings would also provide a venue for NGOs and other sustainability proponents to come together to press for more resolute progress and to forge new collaborations. The Brazilian government offered to host the first of these international assemblies in Rio de Janeiro in June 1992. Modeled to some degree on the Stockholm conference twenty years earlier, the Rio Earth Summit (technically known as the United Nations Conference on Environment and Development, or UNCED) attracted delegations from 178 countries, many led by their heads of state. Also attended by more than 30,000 participants, the Earth Summit generated the Rio Declaration on Environment and Development (a statement of 27 principles undergirding sustainable development), *Agenda 21* (a call to action directed at local governments), and a set of Forest Principles (a nonbinding agreement focused on forest conservation). It additionally led to the establishment of the Commission on Sustainable Development (CSD) (now the United Nations High-Level Political Forum on Sustainable Development (UNHLPFSD)) and the Global Environmental Facility (GEF) (an organizational vehicle for financial assistance to developing countries and countries in transition to support efforts to meet the objectives of international environmental agreements). The Earth Summit moreover led to formalization of three international agreements – the Convention on Biological Diversity (CBD), the United Nations Framework Convention on Climate Change

Table 1.1 Outcomes of Millennium Development Goals

Goal	Target	Outcome	Status
Eradicating poverty and hunger	Halve the proportion of people living on less than $1.25 per day between 1990 and 2015 Achieve decent employment for women, men, and young people Halve the proportion of people who suffer from hunger between 1990 and 2015	Reduced from 1.9 billion in 1990 to 836 million	Achieved poverty target but narrowly missed hunger target
Achieving universal primary education	Ensure that all children can complete a full course of primary schooling, girls and boys by 2015	Net enrollment rate increased from 83% in 2000 to 91% in 2015	Narrowly missed target
Promoting gender equality and empowering women	Eliminate gender disparity in primary and secondary education by 2005, and at all levels by 2015	Approximately two-thirds of developing countries have achieved gender parity in primary education	Significant but not sufficient progress toward target
Reducing child mortality	Reduce by two-thirds the under-5 mortality rate between 1990 and 2015	Child mortality rate declined from 90 deaths per 1,000 live births in 1990 to 43 in 2015 (47% reduction)	Failed to meet target
Improving maternal health	Reduce the maternal mortality ratio by three-quarters between 1990 and 2015	Maternal mortality ratio declined by half	Failed to meet target
Combating HIV/AIDS, malaria, and other diseases	Halt and begin to reverse the spread of HIV/AIDS by 2015 Achieve universal access to treatment for HIV/AIDS for all those who need it Halt and begin to reserve the incidence of malaria and other diseases by 2015	Number of new HIV/AIDS infections declined by 40% between 2000 and 2013	Failed to meet target

Goal	Target	Outcome	Status
Ensuring environmental sustainability	Integrate the principles of sustainable development into country policies and programs and reverse loss of environmental resources Reduce biodiversity loss and achieve a significant reduction in the rate of loss by 2010 Halve the proportion of the population without sustainable access to safe drinking water and basic sanitation	2.6 billion people gained access to improved drinking water between 1990 and 2015 (though 663 million people still lack access to improved drinking water)	Target reached
Forging global partnerships for development	Develop further an open, rule-based, predictable, non-discriminatory trading and financial system Address the special needs of the least developed countries Address the special needs of landlocked developing countries and small island developing states Deal comprehensively with the debt problems of developing countries through national and international measures in order to make debt sustainable in the long term In cooperation with pharmaceutical companies, provide access to affordable, essential drugs in developing countries In cooperation with the private sector, make available the benefits of new technologies, especially information and communications	Overseas development assistance from rich countries to developing countries increased by 66% between 2000 and 2014	Target reached

Source: Achilleas Galatsidas and Finbarr Sheehy, What have the millennium development goals achieved? *Guardian,* July 6, 2015; https://www.un.org/millenniumgoals/.

(UNFCCC; the enabling legal agreement for the Kyoto Protocol and other climate accords), and the United Nations Convention to Combat Desertification (UNCCD).

A subsequent international conference was held in Johannesburg, South Africa in 2002 (officially known as the World Summit on Sustainable Development (WSSD) but generally referred to as Rio+10). The main achievement of the event was the Johannesburg Plan of Implementation (JPI) which outlined a specific timetable for reversing the declining condition of fishery stocks, reducing biodiversity loss, and increasing the share of the global population with access to clean drinking water. Other elements of the JPI included pledges to provide more resources to the CSD and UNEP and further refinement of the process for achieving the Millennium Development Goals (MDGs) (see Table 1.1).

Finally, the third and most recent global sustainability summit (formally known as the United Nations Conference on Sustainable Development (UNCSD)) took place once again in Rio de Janeiro in 2012. Held over ten days and involving upwards of 45,000 people in various capacities, the event included representatives from 192 countries with approximately half of the delegations led by their respective nation's head of state or government. In comparison with the two prior conferences, the objectives for Rio+20 were not clearly articulated and there were no plans for tangible outcomes. The aims centered on securing a renewed commitment to sustainability on the part of national governments and the international community more generally, while assessing progress achieved to date and identifying opportunities for future action.

Given limited expectations in the months leading up to the conference, it was not surprising that the outcomes of Rio+20 were relatively modest. The most significant achievement was affirmation of a short nonbinding working paper entitled *The Future We Want* (United Nations 2012). A consequential element of the report outlined intentions to build on the MDGs and to introduce a new set of sustainability objectives (see below). The conference also initiated a process to enhance the institutional status of UNEP for the first time since its creation in Stockholm in 1972. This initiative entailed the designation of UNEP as "the leading global environmental authority that sets the global environmental agenda, promotes the coherent implementation of the environmental dimension of sustainable development within the United Nations system, and serves as an authoritative advocate for the global environment."[9] Another notable outcome of Rio+20 was the adoption of a ten-year voluntary framework of programs devoted to sustainable consumption and production.

The aftermath of the UNCSD conference has been marked by a combination of frustration and expectation. On the one hand, there is dissatisfaction with the relatively modest results that the process of decadal mega-conferences has produced over the past half-century. After the exuberance of Stockholm and the hopefulness of the first Rio conference, it is clear that subsequent events have not appreciably advanced the global sustainability agenda, and the mixed results of the MDGs are evidence that progress has been unsatisfactory. Indeed, the fact that sizeable amounts of the content in *The Future We Want* was appropriated from *Agenda 21* from twenty years earlier stands, in the minds of many observers, as evidence of the desultory way in which policymakers have, to date, taken up the challenges of sustainability.

On the other hand, significant headway has been made during the post-Rio era to establish a field of sustainability science and to develop a more fully integrated understanding of the essential challenge that begins to give closer parity to poverty and social justice. The United Nations by most measures has mounted a commendable effort to promote a comprehensive framework of Sustainable Development Goals (SDGs) and to reach new audiences through effective dissemination and promotion of its 2030 Agenda.[10] These issues will be discussed in later chapters of this book. An important insight at this stage is that the era of mobilizing popular support for sustainability through large international conclaves has likely reached its end.

Conclusion

With the exception of a few notable moments, there has been, since the dawn of the Industrial Revolution during the middle decades of the eighteenth century, a conspicuous tendency to treat pronouncements of concern about the well-being of humanity and the wider environment as dangerous exaggerations. The pre-industrial artisans whom we remember today as the Luddites sought to resist emergent processes of social and technological change, but were crushed by the British army. Cleric and economist Thomas Malthus, writing at roughly the same time about food scarcity, was criticized for being dour and overly pessimistic. Unfolding processes of industrialization during succeeding years engendered a steady procession of commentators – Henry David Thoreau, Oswald Spengler, Martin Heidegger, Jacques Ellul, E. F. Schumacher, and Ivan Illich – who in often colorful terms questioned the efficacy of continual economic growth and technological advancement.

In due course, environmentalists, too, were derided as either muddled romantics or enemies of progress who failed to appreciate the benefits that flowed from modernization. These denunciations were especially loud and extensive in the settler societies of North America and

Australasia, where conceptions of munificent abundance combined with technoscientific enthusiasm in exceptionally vigorous ways. Particularly since the end of World War II, debates have flared between, on the one hand, unrestrained cornucopians who embrace visions of plentiful and endless bounty and, on the other, detractors of unbridled innovation and expansionism.

Building on the foundations of the *World Conservation Strategy*, the Brundtland Commission sought to bridge this chasm and to bring environmentalism and humanitarianism into mainstream political and economic frameworks. This undertaking required sidestepping customary ecological commitments premised on resource shortages and limits to growth. The intention was that sustainable development could be pursued through adoption of incremental strategies that harmonized apparently competing and irreconcilable societal objectives (Eckersley 2006; Seefried 2015). We could forge so-called win–win solutions to enhance environmental quality, to improve social equity, to foster human well-being, and to bring technological improvements to poorer countries without challenging the central tenets of globalizing industrial-consumer capitalism.

While this uplifting narrative has recruited an avid international coalition of supporters, questions about the relationship between sustainability and customary conceptions of societal progress continue to persist. As we will see in Chapters 2 and 3, for many sustainability specialists, scientific and technological innovation occupies a privileged position with priority attention devoted to achieving engineering break-throughs that simultaneously promise improved resource productivity and enhanced convenience. In later chapters of the book, we will engage the views of commentators who are more measured about exclusive reliance on technical reforms to provide reliable improvements for both people and planet. They advocate instead for a robust array of recommendations that also includes belated social and institutional reforms.

A further challenge is that additional increments of progress – at least in terms of how the concept is currently understood – may prove to be counterproductive. The history of civilization is replete with examples of societies that made notable developmental strides only to discover with the passage of time that these same achievements have given rise to problems beyond their capacity to resolve. Are we facing a similar dilemma today?

In an effort to answer this question, this book will introduce readers to audacious technocratic optimists as well as passionate adherents of "appropriate technology," stalwart champions of localist retrenchment, ardent advocates of economic "degrowth," and numerous others who are unconvinced that the evolutionary arc along which we have been traveling is linear and upward trending. As we undertake this voyage of discovery, it will be important to recognize that sustainability is about formulating responses to urgent issues, but it is also devoted to navigating uncharted waters.

2

The Science of Sustainability

Introduction

Throughout the decades-long period of international conferences, commission reports, and other activities outlined in Chapter 1, researchers were developing corresponding insights. Across the full range of the natural sciences – literally from agronomy to zoology – as well as the social sciences and humanities, sustainability became an important focal point for experimentation and debate. This book does not afford the space to delve into each discipline in detail, but instead traces out key developments pertaining to *global environmental change* that have spurred establishment of the interrelated (and interdisciplinary) fields of sustainability science and Earth system science.

Study of the interactions between the planet's biogeochemical and social systems from the standpoint of sustainability formally began with the Man and the Biosphere (MAB) Programme launched in 1971 by the United Nations Educational, Scientific, and Cultural Organization (UNESCO).[1] This initiative led to a lengthy series of other pursuits, including formation of the World Climate Research Programme (established in 1980), the International Geosphere-Biosphere Programme (IGBP, established in 1987), Diversitas (established in 1991), the International Human Dimensions Programme on Global Environmental Change (established in 1996), and the Earth System Science Partnership (established in 2001). The methodological focus of much of this work centered on remote sensing to investigate land-use changes due to human intrusion, technological mishaps, and other environmental disturbances. NASA in the United States was an important partner in much of this research, largely through its satellite-imaging programs.

Another foundational area of research involved investigations to enhance understanding of the capacity of ecosystems to recover from shocks of various kinds and the impacts of urbanization on hydrological systems, biodiversity, and other natural environments. Also germane was work in the nascent field of sustainability science that explored critical biophysical problems such as climate change, disease vectors, soil toxicity, and air and water pollution (Kates et al. 2001). In addition, research by social scientists centered on the economics of resource use, the contribution of consumption to well-being, the geographic distribution of environmental hazards, and the socioeconomic challenges faced by indigenous populations.

This chapter initially considers three tightly interlocked frameworks that have been developed since the early 2000s and that provide the conceptual foundation of sustainability science – the Anthropocene, planetary boundaries, and the Great Acceleration. The discussion then turns from overarching conceptions to more practical considerations. Specific attention is devoted to how scientists measure whether the global system and its constituent parts are progressing toward a more environmentally tenable and socially equitable future. Consideration is also devoted to the challenge that some of the most critical dimensions of sustainability, most notably issues pertaining to culture and politics, are not readily expressed in numerical terms. The concluding section summarizes the chapter and begins to reconcile the paradox between objectivity and subjectivity in sustainability science.

The Anthropocene

Foundational research in Earth system science and sustainability science has contributed to formulation of the idea that the planet is transitioning into a new period of geological history characterized by pervasive and permanent human influence on natural systems. Termed the Anthropocene, the concept was initially advanced by Paul Crutzen and Eugene Stoermer (2000) and constructed by combining the ancient Greek words *anthropo* (meaning "human") and *–cene* (derived from *kainos* meaning "new") (Davies 2018).[2] Due to its capacity to capture not only the role of climate change but also other sources of ecological disruption, the term generated rapid – and generally positive – reaction

Eon	Era	Period		Epoch	
Phanerozoic	Cenozoic	Quaternary		Holocene	←Present time
					←11,700 years
				Pleistocene	
		Neogene		Pliocene	
				Miocene	
		Paleogene		Oligocene	
				Eocene	
				Paleocene	
					←66 million years
	Mesozoic	Cretaceous			
		Jurassic			
		Triassic			
					←252 million years
	Paleozoic	Permian			
		Carboni-ferous	Pennsylvanian		
			Mississippian		
		Devonian			
		Silurian			
		Ordovician			
		Cambrian			
					←541 million years
Proterozoic					←2500 million years
Archean					←4000 million years
Hadean					←4540 million years

Figure 2.1   Simplified Geologic Time Scale

Source: NASA Advisory Council. (1986). Earth System Science Overview: A Program for Global Change. Washington, DC: NASA.

across a broad cross-section of the scientific community as well as among writers, artists, and others.

A formal proposal to establish the Anthropocene as an official epoch within the familiar Geologic Time Scale (GTS) was submitted in 2008 to the Stratigraphy Commission of the Geological Society of London, the scientific body that makes such determinations (see Figure 2.1).[3] Consideration of this proposition was then referred to the Working Group on the Anthropocene (WGA) of the Subcommission on Quaternary Stratigraphy (of the International Commission on Stratigraphy (ICS) which is itself a constituent part of the International Union of Geological Sciences (IUGS)). The WGA was then charged the following year to begin investigating whether the scope and scale of human-induced impacts on planetary geology and ecosystems have been sufficient to justify this designation. The official administrative process, as well as interest in the topic more widely, has led to numerous research projects to assess the long-term evidence of human activities on soil sedimentology, glacial formation, geomorphology, biogeography, atmospheric chemistry, and other aspects of the biophysical environment.

In 2016, the WGA voted to adopt the Anthropocene as a new geological epoch and this decision triggered a process whereby the ICS Subcommission on Quaternary Stratigraphy and the IUGS will convene their own detailed – and purposefully protracted – processes that will inform decisions on whether to ratify this assessment.

The current version of the GTS identifies the contemporary epoch as the Holocene (meaning "entirely new or recent") which began roughly 11,700 years ago with the end of the last glacial retreat. It follows the Pleistocene and, together, these two epochs comprise the Quaternary period (see Box 2.1). The Holocene is an epoch of geological history that has been notable for its stable climate and biologically favorable conditions. The central argument put forward by proponents of the Anthropocene is that human influences have been disrupting biogeo-chemical systems and generating variability outside the range of relatively conducive conditions that have characterized the Holocene. Climate change has been the most notable source of disturbance, but other factors include biodiversity loss (and biotic mixing and biological homogenization), ocean acidification, and alterations in the nitrogen and phosphorus cycles (see section below on planetary boundaries).

A critical consideration for research and debate centered on the Anthropocene is determining when to establish the onset of the newly proposed epoch, which, according to stratigraphic science, requires a permanent physical imprint in the form of geological evidence (termed stratigraphical signatures or *golden spikes*), typically apparent in fossil records.[4] Because of the relatively recent start date of the Anthropocene (at least according to some determinations; see below for a more complete discussion), it is not generally possible to look for markers of change in rocks and sediments. Rather, scientists refer to more recent physical evidence in the form of so-called *technofossils* which are entirely human-made materials such as concrete, aluminum, and plastics and persistent chemicals like polyaromatic hydrocarbons and polychlorinated biphenyls (Zalasiewicz et al. 2016). Other indicators of the dawn of the Anthropocene include global changes in the nitrogen and phosphorus cycles, atmospheric accumulation of carbon dioxide, radioactive fallout from nuclear weapons detonations, and geographic shifts and extirpations of animal and plant populations. Ecosystem scientist Yadvinder Malhi (2017) provides a comprehensive review of the different schools of thought that extend from deep geologic time to more recent episodes that are within the lifespans of people alive today.

The earliest suggested date for commencement of the Anthropocene is 1–2 million years ago, which corresponds to the early use of fire

---

Box 2.1: Geologic Time Scale

The GTS is a chronological system maintained by the International Commission on Stratigraphy and used to date geologic strata that have developed over 4.6 billion years of Earth history. As shown in Figure 2.1, the standard version of the GTS is divided into eons, eras, periods, and epochs. Accordingly, we are in the midst of the *Phanerozoic eon* (beginning 540 million years ago), the *Cenozoic era* (beginning 66 million years ago), the *Quaternary period* (beginning 2.5 million years ago), and the *Holocene epoch* (beginning 11,700 years ago). The starting date of the Holocene is determined by the end of the most recent glacial retreat.

Human beings have measured geologic time since at least the days of the ancient Greeks, who observed fossils found in rocks. Seashells were the most abundant types and this led early geologists to conclude that proximate land areas were at one time covered by seas. This basic understanding was further developed over the centuries, but early scientific theories were regularly challenged by theological dogma. The first designs of the GTS occurred during the eighteenth century and were based on crude approximations that divided rock types into four periods: primary, secondary, tertiary, and quaternary. Nineteenth-century British geologists were responsible for making the most significant advances to further refine and elaborate the GTS. However, conventional scientific thinking at the time estimated that the age of the Earth was only 1.6 billion years. During the 1970s, stratigraphers formalized the current version of the GTS and established the dating markers in use today.

Source: Timothy Olsen, Benchmarks: March 1913 – The first complete geologic timescale is published. *Earth Magazine*, March 8, 2013; https://www.earthmagazine.org/article/benchmarks-march-1913-first-complete-geologic-timescale-published.

---

by *Homo erectus*. This capability enabled adoption of an increasingly meat-based diet and gave rise to the first evidence of discernible human-caused environmental modification. The proposition for a so-called "early Anthropocene" (also sometimes termed the *Paleoanthropocene*) would actually supersede the Holocene and push the start all the way back to the beginning of the Quaternary period. A similar, though more modest, recommendation calls for setting the onset of the new epoch in accordance with the mass extinction of megafauna that occurred during the late Pleistocene as *Homo sapiens* migrated out of Africa approximately 100,000 years ago. The disappearance of large animals would have resulted in landscape changes that favored forests over grasslands, changed the flow of biogeochemical nutrients, and reduced atmospheric concentrations of methane.

A more popular mid-range proposition is to align the Anthropocene more or less with the Holocene by establishing its onset as the beginning of the Agricultural Revolution that arose in several different global locales approximately 10,000–15,000 years ago and then diffused on a wider geographic scale. These developments led to creation of more sedentary settlements that enhanced the diversity of human diets and increased the anthropogenic greenhouse effect due to rising carbon-dioxide concentrations. More recent proposals for the start of the Anthropocene include the generally simultaneous emergence of large-scale and landscape-altering civilizations such as the Romans and Han Chinese, the European colonial expansion that commenced in the fifteenth century, or the Industrial Revolution that began gathering momentum in approximately 1750. Another proposal contends that the most reliable inception is the mid-twentieth century, as this coincides with the first nuclear tests.

Each of these time perspectives offers certain advantages and disadvantages. For instance, endorsement of an early Anthropocene suggests that (pre-)human modification of the environment is a largely inexorable condition and transcends the features of particular technologies. Accordingly, from this vantage point ecological disruption is an implacable and ageless characteristic of planetary habitation and there is nothing especially unique or urgent about contemporary perturbations. By contrast, setting the beginning of the Anthropocene at the end of World War II (or even the onset of the Industrial Revolution) gives more immediate relevance to the concept but confidently presumes that future events will evolve in accordance with an already conceived trajectory.

In addition to debates centered on the starting date for the Anthropocene and the various sources of biophysical evidence that might support different proposals for when a purported new epoch began, the concept has attracted considerable interest across the full range of the social sciences and humanities, as well as among informed members of the public. Capturing the multifarious uses of the term and its underlying tenets is a difficult undertaking, but one useful taxonomy involves distinguishing between the Anthropocene as a novel cultural outlook, a provocative political challenge, and a new mode of existence. First, as a cultural outlook the concept is an inclusive framework for describing a broad range of environmental challenges, mobilizing societal constituencies behind a common banner, and heralding the need to embrace more sustainable lifestyles. Second, the Anthropocene can be regarded as a kind of politico-environmental manifesto that integrates critiques of capitalism, industrialism, scientific reductionism, and other foundational elements of modernity. Finally, it suggests growing awareness that humanity will need to evolve new ways to think about its place on Earth and to forge innovative practices to avoid transgressing the planet's ecological limits.

Achieving some measure of concurrence on the advent of the Anthropocene also raises questions about how to respond to challenging issues of what the future might hold. One school of thought (discussed in more detail in Chapter 3) is to embrace an ardently managerial mindset and to mobilize our scientific and technological capacities – both current and envisaged – to ensure that human activities do not severely alter or tragically overwhelm biogeochemical processes. A second possible reaction is more pragmatic and stresses the potential to exercise rational stewardship over social and biophysical developments to keep human civilization on a generally upward civilizational arc. We can regard this improvement-oriented perspective as an extension of mainstream conceptions of weak sustainability. A third outlook is decidedly more pessimistic and contends that managerialism and stewardship at this stage are futile. This view asserts that we have already passed critical tipping points and the onset of the Anthropocene marks a distinctive and potentially catastrophic rupture in the planetary system. Humanity accordingly faces a crisis of survival and only transformational change will enable us to avoid societal collapse.

While there are important exceptions, more scientifically conservative commentators have tended to disparage the popularization of the Anthropocene, thus unhelpfully giving public visibility to a highly technical process and conflating science and politics. Colleagues with still more reactionary orientations have ridiculed the very essence of the idea on methodological grounds, charging that it has little serious scientific merit and should be discarded altogether. It is probably accurate to say that these recalcitrant views have become mostly irrelevant in the overall debate. Given the degree to which the concept has been widely embraced, the eventual decision handed down by an august and mostly unaccountable committee of Earth scientists is a matter of negligible importance (Dryzek 2019). The conception of the Anthropocene has diffused into the fabric of society and taken on significance far beyond the institutional contexts that govern the formal scientific debate.

Initial dissemination of the idea is attributable to the fact that it first emerged with an imprimatur of scientific authority, but that distinguished pedigree is less important today. Even without formal ratification by IUGS and its constituent bodies, the Anthropocene will retain influence in the world at large. Growing numbers of people invoke the concept as a kind of shorthand to assert that the impact of humanity, through the application of science and technology of vast power and scope, is having discernible impacts on the planet. In addition to its role as an increasingly common point of reference, the Anthropocene is shaping understanding of how we relate to nature, informing cultural sensibilities, and influencing political developments.

Planetary Boundaries

Building on the idea of the Anthropocene, sustainability scientist Johan Rockström and colleagues (2009) formulated the notion of planetary boundaries (see Figure 2.2). The concept highlights the existence of nine biophysical limits: atmospheric concentration of carbon dioxide, biodiversity loss, anthropogenic movement of nitrogen and phosphorus, ocean acidification, land-use change (primarily from agriculture), human consumption of freshwater, stratospheric ozone depletion, accumulation of particulate matter, and chemical pollution of the environment. Human activities have already transgressed three of these Earth system constraints with respect specifically to the accumulation of greenhouse gases, biodiversity loss, and the nitrogen and phosphorus cycles. Regarding the other boundaries, we are either still within a safe distance of the threshold or there are insufficient data to make a confident determination. The framework is important for its delineation of the outer frontier beyond which environmental impacts are untenable because the biogeochemistry of the planet likely becomes dangerously unstable or the overall system reaches a point where it is unable to reproduce conditions that enable customary forms of life.

The value of the planetary boundaries framework is that, in the words of the authors, "it defines a safe space for human development." Pushing beyond a particular limit raises the potential of reaching a tipping point that prompts a state change in a specific system and precipitates conditions that are both unpredictable and potentially transformative. For instance, increasing greenhouse-gas emissions could trigger a reinforcing feedback loop that accelerates climate change and creates runaway conditions for a "hothouse Earth" that raises sea levels by more than 50 meters. More problematic still are the synergistic and nonlinear effects that could derive from interactions between two or more biogeochemical

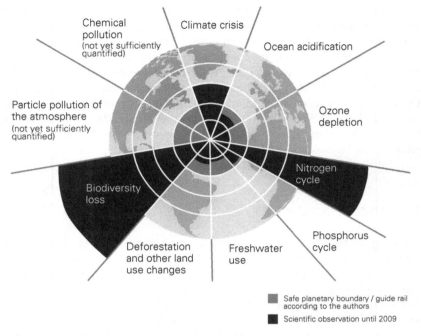

Figure 2.2 Planetary boundaries framework

Source: ©Felix Mueller / Wikimedia Commons / CC-BY-SA-4.0: https://creativecommons. org/licenses/by-sa/4.0/deed.en. Adapted into black and white.

systems that challenge contemporary scientific understanding and could prove extremely unpredictable.

The planetary boundaries have been widely embraced by many global and multilateral governance institutions, including the United Nations and the European Commission, as well as by numerous NGOs. At the same time, they have attracted critical appraisal for understating the degree of complexity (by suggesting that the Earth system can be reduced to discrete limits) and encouraging permissiveness (by suggesting that some thresholds are sufficiently remote that they do not require serious and immediate consideration).

Ecological economist Kate Raworth (2017) has advanced an especially effective critique in the form of an extension to the basic framework (see Figure 2.3). She argues that the planetary boundaries model, because it largely ignores human livelihoods and the existence of pervasive social inequality, amounts to a form of biophysical essentialism. In other words, as initially formulated, the concept is organized around a series of environmental processes and disregards the role that resource

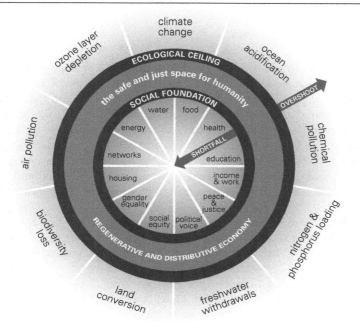

Figure 2.3 Doughnut model

Source: ©User:DoughnutEconomics / Wikimedia Commons / CC-BY-SA-4.0:
https://creativecommons.org/licenses/by-sa/4.0/deed.en. Adapted into black and white.

appropriation plays in meeting basic needs. Termed the Doughnut model, Raworth's idea is that, in addition to biophysical upper limits, sustainability is predicated on ensuring a sufficient social floor below which people should not be allowed to fall. She refers to the space between the planetary maximum and the societal minimum as "the safe and just space for humanity," or the conditions that are required to ensure "inclusive and sustainable economic development." These vital conditions include access to sufficient food, water, and energy; adequate healthcare and education; social equity and gender equality; and availability of jobs and economic opportunities. The unfortunate reality is that not a single country in the world today is situated within this space where conditions of sustainable social and economic welfare are being maintained.

The Great Acceleration

The third concept in this triad of sustainability science frameworks is the Great Acceleration, which highlights the historical connections between changes in global biogeochemical systems and patterns of technoeconomic development (Steffen et al. 2007, 2015). As noted above, dominant conceptions of the Anthropocene place the start of this era during the late eighteenth century and the dawn of the Industrial Revolution. Working from this premise, we can divide this new period of Earth history into a first phase that began roughly in 1800 and lasted until 1945, and second phase that started in 1950 and has persisted until the present.

The first phase of the Anthropocene was marked by rapid increases in the utilization of fossil fuels, initially coal and then petroleum and natural gas. This shift represented a sharp rupture with the past and led to the rapid displacement of wood, water, wind, animal power, and human muscle, which had previously served as primary sources of energy. Development of the technological capacity to exploit these new resources enabled human enterprise to gain access to a vast geological storehouse that, when combined with contemporaneous technological innovations, most notably the steam engine, led to multifold expansion in human population, agricultural production, public health, and the size of the global economy. The resultant impacts in terms of land use (shift from forest to agriculture), hydrology (construction of large dams), and the atmosphere (volume of industrial emissions) were profound.

Though clearly significant as a historical episode, Phase 1 was in many respects only the prologue for the phenomenal developments that followed. Especially noteworthy were the years 1870–1914, which saw momentous economic expansion and the advent of new technologies including automobiles and airplanes. This period established the foundation for an unprecedented growth explosion, though it was not until the aftermath of two devastating wars (1914–18 and 1939–45) and a severe economic depression (beginning in 1929) – including the associated economic and political reorganization that accompanied these tumultuous events – that the truly transformational surge took hold.

The second phase of the Anthropocene, termed the Great Acceleration, began in 1950 as combatant countries began to recover from World War II. The United States, which did not suffer the extent of destruction that leveled large parts of Europe and Japan, was the first country to embark upon this process as it shifted from the manufacture of military supplies to the production of consumer goods. However, it did not take long for other nations to hit their strides. Historians J. R. McNeill and Peter Engelke (2016: 4) capture some of the most significant developments:

> Within the last three human generations, three-quarters of the human-caused loading of the atmosphere with carbon dioxide took place. The number of motor vehicles on Earth increased from 40 million to 850 million. The number of people nearly tripled, and the number of city dwellers rose from about 700 million to 3.7 billion. In 1950, the world produced about 1 million tons of plastics but by 2015 that rose to nearly 300 million tons. In the same time span, the quantities of nitrogen synthesized (mainly for fertilizers) climbed from under 4 million tons to more than 85 million tons.

Researchers working under the purview of the IGBP have divided the factors that enabled the Great Acceleration into two categories. First, the socioeconomic trends include population growth, gross domestic product (GDP), urbanization, fertilizer consumption, and international tourism. A second set of Earth system factors comprises production of nitrous oxide, methane, surface temperature, and tropical forest loss (Steffen et al. 2015). In terms of the vital indicator of atmospheric carbon dioxide, concentrations have increased from 311 parts per million (ppm) in 1950 to 407 ppm in 2018, which is higher than it has been in at least 800,000 years.

The obvious and most critical question for the current age is what the future pattern of the Great Acceleration will be. At least in the affluent countries, the period of exponential growth appears to be ending. Fertility rates have fallen below replacement rate in many of these nations and populations are aging. The pace of technological innovation is slowing and the forcing effects of climate change (in part due to a rise in environmental awareness and increased scientific understanding) may bring the age of fossil fuels to premature closure. Some observers contend that these changes are indications that we are standing on the threshold of the third phase of the Anthropocene, but there is widespread uncertainty how this period will unfold and unanswered questions regarding how we will lift more than 1 billion people out of extreme poverty. Three broadly construed alternatives are possible.

First, the business-as-usual scenario posits that some modest efforts will be made to manage the adverse effects of human activities on the Earth system. Proponents ground their relative optimism in historical examples that demonstrate the capacity of national and local governments to muster sufficient resolve, at least under certain circumstances, to address challenging environmental problems. Adherents of this perspective contend that it may not be possible to offset the full effects of global change, but we ought to be able to forestall the most calamitous impacts. This hopeful prospect, though, carries considerable risk, most notably arising from overly sanguine projections of the effects of climate change and other drivers of instability. Because of the tremendous momentum that is emblematic of the Earth system, if it turns out that actual outcomes are more severe than currently anticipated, it will be too late at that point to implement effective ameliorative action. Particularly catastrophic would be collapse of the Greenlandic ice sheet, which would result in a sea-level rise in excess of 6 meters. The inundation would displace an estimated 85 million people in China, 32 million in Vietnam, and 28 million in India (Dutton 2015; Kahn 2015).

Second, a mitigation scenario seeks to mobilize a wave of technological innovation – in combination with modified social practices and new cultural values – to set humanity on a different civilizational trajectory. The expectation is that this commitment would be sufficient to keep sources of destabilization within manageable bounds and thus reduce pressure on the Earth system to levels that would avoid the most serious effects of global change. Tremendous opportunities exist to reduce wasteful consumption, to harness a larger share of solar radiation, to restore ecosystems, to dematerialize production, and to shift mobility practices to more energy-efficient modes. However, for this strategy to be effective there is little time for delay. Without prompt action, it will likely not be possible to dial back the velocity that has built up during the Great Acceleration.

Finally, in the face of severe consequences brought on by rising green-house-gas emissions and other sources of global instability, it would be difficult to avoid embarking on intensive management of the planet. Discussed in more detail in Chapter 3, this highly controversial portfolio of so-called geoengineering (or Earth system engineering) strategies involves active and direct human manipulation of biophysical processes through, for instance, reversing adverse changes in ocean chemistry by adding iron or capturing carbon dioxide for storage in geological formations.

Measuring Sustainability

The previously described outlooks about the Anthropocene are instructive for Earth system scientists and allied researchers focused on large-scale processes of global environmental change. These frameworks are important because they put the challenges of sustainability into a broad context and demonstrate the formidable scope of the challenges that humanity currently faces. However, policymakers and practitioners tend to encounter a different set of dilemmas as they seek to under-stand the societal and environmental impacts of distinct practices and to ameliorate the consequences of untoward human activities. It is commonly said that "only what gets measured gets managed" and there is surely considerable truth to this adage. The implication is that in a world with an essentially limitless number of problems, it is typically necessary to summon quantitative data that places specific issues in bold relief. It is oftentimes additionally crucial to demonstrate statistical relationships between cause and effect as well as to delineate how proposed interventions might differently contribute to beneficial course correction. This section surveys several of the most common metrics used to assess the direction that societies are moving in with respect to sustainability targets. The discussion is organized into three overarching frameworks: biophysical, socioeconomic, and integrated.

Biophysical sustainability metrics

It merits noting that measurement of the Earth system does not generally lend itself to laboratory experimentation under controlled settings. Sustainability scientists must typically work in extreme environments and under highly dynamic conditions. The collection of data can be expensive and requires the organization of large teams that need to collaborate over extended periods. Not infrequently, the most comprehensive datasets are compiled by government agencies and commitment ebbs and flows based on electoral outcomes. Even when responsibility is devolved to other organizations, public funds are often necessary to ensure successful execution. Because sustainability is as much a political pursuit as it is a technological and scientific undertaking, the mobilization of resources for data collection, analysis, and dissemination inevitably takes place within a context of civic and legislative negotiation.

For example, governments did not begin to measure – and more importantly publicize – the size and growth rates of their domestic economies until after they could confidently ensure results that enhanced political success. Until that day arrived during the 1950s and 1960s, the calculation of national accounts was mostly an arcane exercise performed outside the purview of public attention (Applebaum 2019). Similarly, in the United States prior to the passage of the Emergency Planning and Community Right-to-Know Act of 1986 and the Pollution Prevention Act of 1990 (which were responses to a series of high-profile environmental accidents), few industrial corporations kept comprehensive records of their ambient emissions of toxic chemicals. This legislation established a Toxic Release Inventory (TRI) to serve as a source of public information so that local communities could apply coercive pressure on the managers of polluting facilities to improve their environmental operations.

These data also increasingly were used for management decision-making as it became apparent that cost savings could be achieved by making relatively minor adjustments in chemical formulations that reduced the volume of byproducts that needed to be discarded through incineration or other means. In due course, this knowledge led to elaborate methodologies, specifically life-cycle analysis (LCA), which is a mathematical tool for tracking energy and material inputs across the full range of a production process – extraction, fabrication, assembly, utilization, and disposal (as well as the transportation linkages that are part of supply chains). Software systems and associated algorithms have been commercially developed to standardize the preparation of LCAs and most industrial companies deploy them as part of environmental management systems (EMSs) to identify opportunities to enhance the efficiency of production processes. A shortcoming is that analysts often deploy these procedures for narrowly instrumental reasons – such as increasing quarterly earnings – and they ultimately convey a false sense of scientific precision. It can also be notoriously difficult to assemble the full range of necessary data and even those that are available may be of limited or even dubious quality.

Some analysts have developed extensions of conventional LCA methodologies that seek to correct these limitations and to account for wider societal impacts. Two prominent examples are social LCA and life-cycle sustainability analysis, but these procedures have to date not been widely adopted. Researchers have also combined LCA with input–output analysis (a methodology for using matrix algebra to model flows between industrial sectors).

At the societal scale, there has been a longstanding concern – traceable at least as far as publication of the 1972 *Limits to Growth* report – about the scale of human impacts on the Earth system relative to the productive capacity of the planet. The Dutch economist J. B. Opschoor developed a scientific framework for analyzing this prospect that he termed *environmental space* (in Dutch *milieugebruiks-ruimte*, which literally means "environmental utilization space"). The concept was defined as "limits to the amount of environmental pressure that the Earth's ecosystems can handle without irreversible damage to these systems or to the life support processes that they enable" (Hille 1997).

Building on this notion and borrowing some techniques from LCA, ecological economists William Rees and Mathis Wackernagel (1996) developed an accounting tool called ecological footprint analysis (EFA). The EFA measures human demands on the Earth system in terms of both the appropriation of resources and the disposal of wastes. The Global

Footprint Network (GFN) calculates the amount of natural capital that is annually required to maintain human livelihoods both for the planet as a whole and for different global subpopulations. Current trends indicate that humanity is using biospheric capacity at 1.7 times the rate at which the Earth is able to renew it.

Calculation of the ecological footprint involves determining the number of hectares required to provide for the sequestration of carbon dioxide and the resources that are utilized to provide for food, housing, and other goods and services. According to GFN, the size of the global footprint increased from 7 billion hectares in 1961 to 20.6 billion hectares in 2014. Average per capita ecological footprints are closely correlated with income per person and range from 15.8 hectares in Luxembourg and 10.8 hectares in Qatar to 0.61 hectares in Haiti, 0.49 in Eritrea, and 0.48 in Timor-Leste. The global average is 2.7 hectares per person.[5]

A related methodology involves calculation of volumes of total material consumption (TMC) relative to globally available supplies. An early approximation formulated during the 1990s by industrial ecologist Friedrich Schmidt-Bleek, founder of the Factor 10 Institute, estimated an annual budget of 4–5 metric tons per person (mt/p). During the following decade, Stefan Bringezu calculated that yearly abiotic resource appropriation needed to decrease from an average of 16–18 mt/p to 5.6–6.1 mt/p. More recent estimates by Bringezu (2009) distinguish between three separate material flows and he proposes the following as yearly sustainable TMC levels: abiotic resources of 6–12 mt/p, biotic resources not in excess of 2 mt/p, and used biotic and abiotic resources of 3–6 mt/p. Despite efficiency improvements, TMCs for high-income countries continue to increase and are presently estimated to be 40–50 mt/p (Lettenmeier et al. 2014; Wiedmann et al. 2015).

Still other means of measuring sustainability have long been part of the toolkit used by environmental scientists. For instance, atmospheric chemists, hydrologists, and toxicologists regularly track the deposition and accumulation of pollutants in the air, soil, water, and human bodies using high-precision instruments. In addition, as the availability of fresh-water has become an increasing concern in parts of the world such as the Himalayan watershed (in part as a result of climate change, which is changing patterns of rainfall and snowmelt), new methodologies for forecasting alternative future scenarios have been developed at the interface of meteorology, hydrological science, and other specialties. However, these models have high levels of uncertainty due to the prevalence of synergistic effects and the inability to predict how future political events might contribute to changes in usage patterns. It has also been conceptually difficult to connect these biophysical measures with socioeconomic data in rigorous ways, though researchers have begun to make some important advances in demonstrating the equity implications of different endowments of natural capital (Daneshvar et al. 2018). In addition, the notion of climate justice has entered into contemporary discussions of the distributional effects of rising greenhouse-gas emissions and has increasingly become a factor in assessments (Mera et al. 2015; Alcaraz et al. 2018).

Socioeconomic sustainability metrics

No one single metric is likely to be sufficient to determine whether we are moving positively toward a more sustainable future either at the global level or within specific geographic locales (Böhringer and Jochem 2007). The challenge is akin to the ancient South Asian parable of the blind men and the elephant. This famous allegory tells the story of how each individual places his hands on a different part of the beast and generalizes from his own tactile experience. One fellow touches a tusk and claims that the large animal is similar to a snake. Another blind man examines a leg and confidently reports that it is a sturdy pillar. And so on.

It is for this reason that it has become increasingly common to formulate composites of indicators that provide a more complete picture of current conditions and emergent trends (Heal 2012). A particularly well-known example is the Human Development Index (HDI) designed by Nobel laureate Amartya Sen and popularized by the United Nations Development Programme (UNDP). The index combines three constituent elements (on an unweighted basis): life expectancy, educational achievement, and per capita income. The top five countries on this measure in 2018 were Norway, Switzerland, Australia, Ireland, and Germany. The United States and the United Kingdom, respectively, were in thirteenth and fourteenth positions. The lowest ranked countries were all located in sub-Saharan Africa and comprised Burundi, Chad, South Sudan, the Central African Republic, and Niger (UNDP 2018).

The HDI, though, is relatively distinctive because its champions held firm on expanding the indicators beyond the currently modest number. In other areas of practice, there has been a tendency to resolve conflicts among competing perspectives by allowing the elements of the index to become overly large. Instead of a succinct calculation that provides relatively unambiguous policy advice, an alternative has often been to include dozens (or even hundreds) of indicators. This complexity inevitably makes it difficult to draw conclusions about general patterns amidst the welter of detail and conflicting evidence. In addition, as Böhringer and Jochem (2007) usefully explain, many composite indicators fail basic tests of scientific reliability because of incommensurate aggregation, lack of adequate transparency, and tendencies to employ ad hoc techniques regarding normalization. Some of these problems have been mitigated by the creation of dashboards that function like the control panel of a car and simultaneously provide real-time information (often color-coded) on several sustainability metrics.

Another way around this dilemma of how best to balance comprehensiveness with practicality has been to formulate so-called indicative indicators based on meta-scale conceptual conditions like resource consumption, human well-being, or happiness (Tatzel 2013; Lepenies 2019). The widely referenced notion of Gross National Happiness (GNH) is an example of this technique and the South Asian nation of Bhutan has achieved considerable notoriety over the last few years for adopting GNH as national policy framework (Bok 2010). The Bhutanese formulation is predicated on nine factors: psychological well-being, time use, community vitality, culture, health, education, environmental diversity, living standard, and governance. However, in international comparisons Bhutan's ranking is inconsistent with the attention it has received. For instance, in the World Happiness Report released in 2019 by the Center for Sustainable Development at Columbia University and several collaborating institutions, the country was in 95th place. The happiest countries in the world in this study were Finland, Denmark, Norway, Iceland, and the Netherlands (Helliwell et al. 2019). A different study carried out by the New Economics Foundation (2016) and entitled the Happy Planet Index (HPI) identified Costa Rica, Mexico, Colombia, Vanuatu, and Vietnam as the happiest countries in the world.

Another indicative alternative is to rely on metrics that are based on longitudinal analysis and can serve as proxy measures for more complex processes of social change. In the biophysical realm, greenhouse-gas emissions have come to serve this purpose, while socially the rate of female empowerment – especially through the availability of resources to enhance capacity for family planning – is frequently used to highlight developments regarded as consistent and supportive of sustainability more generally (Parris and Kates 2003). These are all notable efforts, but none of these metrics rivals GDP, which exerts singular and virtually unchallenged influence on macroeconomic policymaking and public understanding of general economic conditions. The GDP is a measure of the total monetary value of all goods and services produced in a region – typically a country – over the course of a year. It is calculated by summing aggregate consumption, total investment, government spending, and net imports/exports. The media regularly trumpets changes in GDP on a monthly basis and expressed in per capita terms it is arguably the primary means used to gauge the status of nations. Countries that are growing more slowly than forecasts or in comparison to their peers are judged to be performing poorly. Most prominent in this regard has been Japan which observers have derisively branded, because of its relatively low and occasionally negative GDP growth rate, to be a pitiable under-achiever. By contrast, for most of the past twenty years China has had a GDP growth rate of approximately 10 percent and has accordingly grown far more prosperous over time. The countries with the highest per capita GDP in 2018 as calculated by the IMF were Qatar ($130,475), Luxembourg ($106,705), Singapore ($100,345), Brunei ($79,530), and Ireland ($78,785).

Nonetheless, from a sustainability perspective, GDP is a very fraught and problematic measure. It perversely treats the perpetuation of environmental destruction and social decay as positive contributions to the overall sum because these activities typically entail, in one way or another, the purchase of goods and services and the resultant exchange of money (see Box 2.2). Upward movement of the metric can oftentimes mask the fact that human well-being and overall quality of life is declining for vast numbers of people at the same time that the economy, at least in crudely quantitative terms, is growing. These flaws have long been recognized and even Simon Kuznets, the economist who designed the system of national accounts on which GDP is based, famously remarked in 1934: "The welfare of a nation can scarcely be inferred from a measurement of national income." There has to date been entrenched resistance to its replacement, though there has recently been progress in some countries to establish and publicize so-called distributional national accounts that assess how GDP is allocated across different income cohorts (Stiglitz et al. 2010; Piketty et al. 2018). More ambitious is the work of ecological economists, sustainability scientists, and others to develop various alternatives that make systemic correc-tions for the deep-rooted flaws in how economic well-being is generally assessed (Philipsen 2015).

From the more conservative side of the spectrum there have been calls for reform premised on the use of net domestic product (NDP) (which merely aims to include fair values for depreciation of capital assets) and adjusted net savings (ANS) (which builds on NDP by including investment in human capital and changes in the value of natural capital) (Heal 2012). At the more progressive end, various efforts to "green" GDP aim to systematically identify the costs associated with economic activities that impair the environment or reduce social capital (Pilling 2018). Such metrics also add investments in ecological improvement or contributions to societal betterment, but may not have monetary

Box 2.2: Robert F. Kennedy's 1968 speech at the University of Kansas

Just a few months before he was assassinated in June 1968, US Senator Robert F. Kennedy (brother of former President John F. Kennedy) delivered a speech at the University of Kansas decrying the use of Gross National Product (which had some minor methodological differences with GDP and was the prevalent metric used in the United States until 1991).

Even if we act to erase material poverty, there is another greater task, it is to confront the poverty of satisfaction – purpose and dignity – that afflicts us all. Too much and for too long, we seemed to have surrendered personal excellence and community values in the mere accumulation of material things. Our Gross National Product, now, is over $800 billion dollars a year, but that Gross National Product – if we judge the United States of America by that – that Gross National Product counts air pollution and cigarette advertising, and ambulances to clear our highways of carnage. It counts special locks for our doors and the jails for the people who break them. It counts the destruction of the redwood and the loss of our natural wonder in chaotic sprawl. It counts napalm and counts nuclear warheads and armored cars for the police to fight the riots in our cities. It counts Whitman's rifle and Speck's knife, and the television programs which glorify violence in order to sell toys to our children. Yet the gross national product does not allow for the health of our children, the quality of their education or the joy of their play. It does not include the beauty of our poetry or the strength of our marriages, the intelligence of our public debate or the integrity of our public officials. It measures neither our wit nor our courage, neither our wisdom nor our learning, neither our compassion nor our devotion to our country, it measures everything in short, except that which makes life worthwhile. And it can tell us everything about America except why we are proud that we are Americans.

Source: John F. Kennedy Library and Museum; https://www.jfklibrary. org/learn/about-jfk/the-kennedy-family/robert-f-kennedy/robert-f-kennedy-speeches/remarks-at-the-university-of-kansas-march-18-1968.

values associated with the relevant activities. Examples include volunteer programs to protect biodiversity or to renew the social fabric of communities. The most popular applications of this approach include the Index of Sustainable Economic Welfare (ISEW), the Genuine Progress Indicator (GPI), and the Living Planet Index (LPI) (Mori and Christodoulou 2012).

Integrated sustainability metrics

An emergent means of analysis involves combining biophysical and socioeconomic metrics into more systemic frameworks, typically as a way to contrast and categorize the sustainability performance of different countries. An especially instructive formulation developed by GFN involves assessing the correlation between per capita ecological footprint and the HDI. When examined in such terms, nations of the world, likely unsurprisingly, tend to cluster into two groups – high ecological footprint/high HDI (high-income consumer countries) and low ecological footprint/low HDI (low-income agrarian countries).

This sorting demonstrates the generally close relationship between resource consumption and human development. High-income consumer countries include the United States, Sweden, and the Netherlands, though there are important differences between them. Most low-income agrarian countries are located in sub-Saharan Africa and the Asia-Pacific region, though here, too, there are significant variations. Notably, no country in the world today combines a low ecological footprint with a high HDI, which would be emblematic of a largely sustainable nation.

Somewhat more optimistically, a related integrated sustainability metric contrasts per capita ecological footprint and happiness. This correlation reveals that Costa Rica and Colombia are not far outside of what we could regard as sustainable development. This determination suggests that the objective is within reach and exemplar countries can serve as useful case studies on how to combine modest resource consumption with high levels of well-being and life satisfaction.

Also instructive is the interpretation of these frameworks for combining biophysical and socioeconomic measures as a certain kind of efficiency metric. The point is not to refer to efficiency as it is customarily understood, namely as the rate at which resources (materials, energy, labor, capital) are converted into output. Rather, achievement of a high HDI (or happiness score) and a relatively low per capita ecological footprint suggest that a country has robust capacity to effectively convert resource endowments into welfare-enhancing goods and services. By contrast, a low HDI and a comparatively high per capita ecological footprint suggest weak societal efficiency. Numerous reasons

– inadequate investment in education and healthcare, insufficient legal structures, widespread corruption, and so forth – might be responsible for an unfavorable "resources-to-wellbeing conversion rate" and cross-national comparisons can be the start of an exploratory process to pinpoint the source of underlying deficiencies.

Final considerations on sustainability metrics

It needs to be noted that the foregoing discussion provides a survey of the use of metrics for assessing sustainability at the level of whole societies, which as a practical matter generally tends to mean the country scale. Sustainability scientists have also developed various frameworks to evaluate major cities on a range of indicators, though the procedures used to carry out these assessments are quite diverse and users need to be attentive to the underlying methodologies. One noteworthy example is the ranking compiled by Arcadis (2016), an international design consultancy, which identifies the top five "overall most sustainable cities" as Zurich, Singapore, Stockholm, Vienna, and London. However, there is considerable variability across this group when the cities are examined in terms of their more detailed social, environmental, and economic features. Other chapters in this book discuss a number of additional issues that suggest we should be careful in reading too much into these results.

Furthermore, specific fields of sustainability policy and practice – ranging from architecture to agriculture to industrial supply chains – have developed measurement tools specially customized for their own purposes. For instance, the building industry has formulated certification schemes such as Leadership in Energy and Environmental Design (LEED) and Building Research Establishment Environmental Assessment Method (BREEAM). Similarly, countries and multilateral confederations (such as the European Union) have created accreditation programs for evaluating the energy efficiency of refrigerators, televisions, and so forth. In the United States, Energy Star™ is a relatively familiar program for rating the annual energy use and average cost of a wide range of household appliances, although it should be noted that relevant trade associations have played influential roles in developing the standards, and this situation has led to an emphasis on technical rather than actual performance (Shove 2018; Rinkinen et al. 2019). For instance, building certifications typically do not involve meaningful post-occupancy assessment and system efficiencies can deviate sharply from expectations (Leaman and Bordass 2007; Meir et al. 2009). Moreover, the social dimensions of sustainability are generally omitted from these procedures and the design objective is confined to reducing energy consumption only on a per-unit basis (for instance per cubic foot of refrigerated space), rather than for the overall appliance.

Can We Really Measure Sustainability?

It is important to recognize that some sustainability experts dismiss the need to formulate metrics and contend that a more environmentally tenable and socially equitable world cannot be achieved by single-minded reliance on quantitative assessment. This perspective suggests that sustainability is too multifariously complex and is not reducible to a single number, or even an array of dashboard indicators. Indeed, no less a champion of improvement through quantitative analysis, celebrated management expert W. Edward Deming, observed that it is a myth to suppose that measurement is a prerequisite for sound and effective managerial control (Harris and Tayler 2019). The forsaking of numerical appraisal is premised on an expansive vision of social change and a worldview that contends that the most important objectives are not amenable to measurement.

From this provocative standpoint, there are at least three reasons why we should be circumspect about relying too heavily on sustainability metrics. First, singular commitment to quantifiable rubrics can lead to "paralysis by analysis" (Karvonen and Brand 2007; Longo et al. 2019). Different diagnostic techniques will often generate varying, and perhaps even contradictory, results. Such circumstances can quite reasonably lead to efforts to seek out even more data and still more powerful tools under the presumption that higher caliber quantification can resolve outstanding conflicts. However, this approach is likely to produce even more confounding confusion and uncertainty. While numerical formulation can often provide instructive guidance, in most policy debates it is not an adequate substitute for prudent judgment.

Second, sustainability cannot be achieved through the accumulation of quantitative evidence and strategic management because it is fundamentally about changing societal norms and cultural mindsets. Transition at this meta-scale level is unachievable on the basis of incremental planning and rational policymaking; rather, it requires a revolutionary break with increasingly outmoded practices and thinking and the emergence of more pro-environmental and pro-social ethical sensibilities (Almlund and Jespersen 2012; Dhiman and Marques 2016). Consistent with this idea is the growing popularity of mindfulness as a technique to encourage through positive psychology the emergence of new conceptions about the relationship between humanity and the Earth system (Ericson et al. 2014).

Finally, reticence to embrace the measurement of sustainability stems from a more epistemological argument, namely that it is folly to presume that we can apply objectivist scientific tools to our current predicament (Capra 1984; Toulmin 1992). We must instead recover a prior (in some cases pre-Enlightenment) commitment to humanist values that embrace rather than reject morality and ethics.

Conclusion

Humanity has long struggled to adapt its activities to biophysical constraints and several contemporary ideas regarding management of this relationship have ancient origins. But it was not until the 1970s that research on interactions between society and the Earth system emerged as a formal area of inquiry. Over the following decades, initial conceptual formulations coalesced and combined with political developments to give rise to the discernible field of sustainability science. Important conceptual advancements in recent years have centered on seminal frameworks such as the Anthropocene, planetary boundaries, and the Great Acceleration.

An enduring quandary in sustainability science is the efficacy of measurement. There is widespread recognition that empirical investigation requires quantification, and particularly mathematical and computational modeling of complex systems. Metrics are necessary to accumulate and organize knowledge and to inform policymakers and others about changes in environmental and social conditions. At the same time, many researchers contend that critical aspects of the human condition are not readily reducible to numerical assessment. Under such circumstances, sustainability scientists seek to combine the rigors of the scientific method with an appreciation of cultural differences and varying social aspirations, as well as awareness that subjectivity and normativity are inescapable elements of professional practice.

Reconciliation of this paradox resides in acknowledging that sustainability science is not a science in the same sense as physics or chemistry. Researchers in these more customary fields can generally conduct their work in controlled settings and without active involvement of societal stakeholders. Sustainability science, by contrast, requires the fusing of different disciplinary knowledges and the mobilizing of biophysical and social evidence in collaboration with political institutions and the general public. It also involves integration with more humanistic forms of understanding that are sensitive to diverse historical experiences. The concept of transdisciplinarity describes a process of knowledge creation which involves the integration of scientific and non-scientific perspectives. Central to its effective implementation is high tolerance of ambiguity and multiple ways of understanding and mutual respect for contested and competing points of view. We are at the very early stages of apprehending how to conduct meaningful and effective research based on transdisciplinary principles, but sustainability science is at the forefront of these efforts. The issue is explored further in later chapters of this book.

3

Engineering a More Sustainable Future

Introduction

Al Gore, former US vice-president and long-time climate-change champion, summarized a series of familiar travails arising from the increasing accumulation of greenhouse-gas emissions: the growing number of Category 5 hurricanes, the rise in destructive forest fires, the collapse of the Greenlandic ice sheet, and so forth. He then observed:

> We have the technology we need ... solar and wind provide the cheapest sources of new electricity in two-thirds of the world. Within five more years, these sources are expected to provide the cheapest new electricity in the entire world. And in 10 years, solar and wind electricity will be cheaper nearly everywhere than the electricity that existing fossil fuel plants will be able to provide. (Gore 2019)

While setting aside for the moment the fact that sustainability entails more than reducing the installation costs of renewable energy technologies, it merits pausing to acknowledge more generally the extent to which these sentiments about the efficacy of technology are manifest. Indeed, for many people sustainability is tantamount to unleashing the creativity of our most formidable engineering minds and tethering their ideas to innovative business models. For a variety of reasons, this is an alluring vision. It is based on a conception that, beyond a few carefully targeted tax incentives and some limited regulatory oversight, we do not need to strain the limited capacity of government and it is unnecessary for anyone to make any burdensome and disagreeable sacrifices.

History has repeatedly demonstrated that capitalist societies are equipped with an extremely powerful engine for social transformation and the primary obstacle at present, implicit in Gore's confident forecasts, is that, when the business community seizes on a problem and identifies a technological solution, it can change the world. He further proceeds to observe that we underestimate the potential of these capabilities at our peril and quotes the famous adage of MIT economist Rudiger Dornbusch: "Things take longer to happen than you think they will, but then they happen much faster than you thought they could."[1]

In the face of untoward societal challenges, this advice provides a kind of understated reassurance. We do not need to launch courageous and ultimately unpredictable crusades aimed at achieving political upheaval or sweeping changes in cultural norms. The overall transition is essentially, counterintuitive though it may seem, a supercharged version of the status quo and we can dig ourselves out of danger if we just keep our anxieties in check. We just need to reorient our current institutions in a better direction and, with a little good fortune, the whole undertaking could fortuitously prove quite lucrative for well-positioned entrepreneurs.

The frontier for ostensibly sustainable technologies is not limited, of course, to just photovoltaics and wind turbines. The engineered vision of a less ecologically and socially damaging future also includes autonomous vehicles, next-generation nuclear power, biofuels, genetically modified foods, vertical farms, hydrogen-powered water-desalination plants, and much more. Sustainability scientists, for their part, have developed the term "ecological modernization" to describe this worldview, and this chapter first examines the tenets of this conceptual framework. The discussion then considers, in the sections that follow, how so-called "ecomodernist" tenets are being applied to address real-world problems. We then turn to strategic questions of whether it makes sense to put all our sustainability eggs into engineering baskets. The conclusion provides some cautionary recommendations for carefully considering the potential of exclusive reliance on engineered solutions and highlights the need to pursue a more comprehensive range of options.

The Theory of Ecological Modernization

The contours of the theory of ecological modernization were first traced out during the 1980s by a group of German social scientists that principally included Joseph Huber, Martin Jänicke, Udo Simonis, and Ernst von Weizsäcker. They contended that presumed conflicts between economic priorities and environmental quality were manifestations of a false choice. Industrial firms could simultaneously foster economic growth and protect natural resources, and, in particular, upgraded materials and energy efficiencies and new environmental technologies represented important opportunities for product innovation, improved productivity, and market expansion. The pathway for achieving these objectives included implementation of new managerial tools, including EMSs, eco-auditing, and LCA (see Chapter 2). Through application of these informational lenses, firms could identify opportunities to enhance resource allocations, to replace toxic substances with more benign (and oftentimes cheaper) alternatives, and to design less polluting manufacturing processes. The role of government would not be that of an enforcement agent, but rather a stern but supportive coach, urging better performance through a combination of customized advice and carefully scripted regulations.

The expectation is that aggregation of efforts by numerous companies and other organizations across a national economy would lead to systemic transformation due to newly reinvigorated research programs and enhanced economic competitiveness. In short, society would transcend its environmental problems and launch itself on a new phase of modernization. In this sense, ecological modernization is the third stage of a process of civilizational progression that began with agricultural modernization, advanced with industrial modernization, and reaches culmination through widespread support for environmental reform. Viewed from this vantage point, ecological modernization shares some notable similarities with other prominent conceptual frameworks. Most notable is Nikolai Kondratiev's (1935) long wave theory, Walt Rostow's (1960) linear stage theory of economic growth, and the environmental Kuznets curve (Selden and Song 1994; named for economist Simon Kuznets), which all privilege the role of technology as the primary driver of societal advancement.

Further elaborations of this basic conception were carried out first by several Dutch social scientists and then by a larger international community of researchers (Spaargaren and Mol 1992; Hajer 1995). These perspectives widened the focus beyond business and industrial innovation and developed a more expansive sociological view that included NGOs, consumers, and social movements. These extensions of the basic theory of ecological modernization also suggested that it was necessary not only to focus on processes of environmental reform but also to consider related dynamics associated with the modernization of the political system.

A summary presentation of the theory of ecological modernization begins by noting that a forthcoming industrial revolution will catalyze a series of advanced environmental technologies. The deployment of this equipment and associated expertise will correct the "design flaws" (pollution and other forms of overexploitation of resources) associated with industrial modernity. Moreover, these innovations will be fundamentally different from the sorts of largely end-of-pipe and ameliorative approaches that preceded them. This new generation of advanced techniques will fundamentally transform production systems by eliminating waste and achieving several-fold improvements in energy and materials efficiencies. Ultimately, economic growth will be "decoupled" from environmental performance and value added will increase while simultaneously reducing resource inputs.

Countries at the forefront of earlier industrial revolutions were able to achieve comparative ("first mover") advantages, and nations that are the pioneers during the emergent era of ecological modernity will realize similar benefits (Porter and van der Linde 1995). Importantly, calls for a "new industrial revolution" mean that, contrary to some environmental strategies that are deemed to be backward looking and centered on scarcity and biophysical limits, ecological modernization is unequivocally premised on assertively and optimistically moving into a bright future of abundance.

Applying the Tenets of Ecological Modernization

Ecological modernization is not just a conceptual framework for environmental reform and associated modes of social change. This mode of thinking has, in important ways, informed development of the field of industrial ecology, which brings together elements of environmental engineering and environmental science to focus on the symbiotic design of industrial processes (or metabolisms) to create material cascades where the waste of one stage of production serves as the feedstock for other activities. Instituted on a sufficiently comprehensive basis, it becomes possible for companies to eliminate nonmarketable byproducts and the concept can be applied even more widely at the scale of "eco-industrial parks" whereby firms co-locate in close proximity to conveniently access recycling and reuse networks. The most famous example is in the Danish city of Kalundborg, which is home to numerous manufacturing operations that participate in a highly integrated system of waste exchange.

The principles of ecological modernization are also evident in the field of ecological design and specifically in the notion of "cradle-to-cradle" widely popularized by architect William McDonough and environmental chemist Michael Braungart (McDonough and Braungart 2002, 2013). This mode of industrial practice involves distinguishing materials as being part of either the "biosphere" or the "technosphere." On the one hand, resources that are constituent elements of the former are derived from nature and, when disposed, will safely biodegrade. On the other hand, materials that are part of the technosphere – such as metals and plastics – need to be separately managed and ideally should be fabricated from their inception in ways that ensure maximum recyclability.

While ecological modernization is predominant within the engineering professions, it is also widespread, though in perhaps less emphatic form, in society more generally. We can call this particular mindset "soft ecological modernization." The writer David Owen captures its essence when he says that for most people sustainability "is living pretty much the way that I live right now, though maybe with a different car."[2] We could discuss the adequacy of this mode of thinking (and we will do so in Chapters 4 and 5), but for the time being it is sufficient to simply take note of the prevalence of technocentric thinking in contemporary discussions of sustainability. Two especially prominent organizational exponents of ecological modernization are Rocky Mountain Institute and Breakthrough Institute, whose work is explained in Boxes 3.1 and 3.2.

Box 3.1: Amory Lovins and Rocky Mountain Institute

Physicist Amory Lovins first received acclaim during the energy crises of the 1970s when he popularized the proposition of a "soft energy path." This alternative trajectory was predicated on a combination of renewable sources and energy efficiency, and it differed dramatically from dominant thinking of the time based on expansion of fossil-fuel supplies (the "hard energy path"). Such ideas resonated closely with the campaigns of environmental organizations at the time and contributed to an insurgent policy agenda. A key political implication was that the soft energy path would reduce the need for direct and indirect military engagement to protect vulnerable supply lines required to maintain the global system for transporting oil.

Lovins was also an early voice in identifying the problem of excessive accumulation of carbon dioxide in the atmosphere due to the burning of fossil fuels and the inseparability between civilian nuclear energy for electricity production and proliferation of bomb-making capabilities. Another keen insight was his recognition that energy is not valued as a commodity in and of itself. He asserted that people instead derive benefits from its utilization and are indifferent to the source from which it is derived. Lovins coined the adage that we do not care about energy as such, but for the services that it delivers in the form of hot showers and cold beer. He also promoted the notion that investments in energy efficiency constituted a "lunch that you are paid to eat" (as opposed to the more sullen but nonetheless common view that "there is no thing as a free lunch").

In 1982, Lovins (together with Hunter, his wife at the time) founded Rocky Mountain Institute (RMI), a think-tank and innovation laboratory headquartered amidst the snow-capped mountains of Colorado. RMI today employs more than 200 engineers and other staff members who work on consulting projects for Fortune 500 companies and the American military. The Institute's activities are described as "independent and non-adversarial" and it places strong emphasis on market-driven solutions to contemporary environment and energy problems. RMI has pioneered a number of disruptive technologies, including the Hypercar, a superefficient automobile that combines streamlined design with ultralight materials, and a plug-in hybrid vehicle that achieves 100 miles per gallon. RMI is also involved in projects in China and India, and is seeking to propel transportation technologies that leapfrog to electric vehicles.

Source: Rocky Mountain Institute website: https://rmi.org. Heather Clancy, High aspirations: What's next for Rocky Mountain Institute? *GreenBiz*, October 23, 2017; https://www.greenbiz.com/article/high-aspirations-whats-next-rocky-mountain-institute.

Box 3.2: Breakthrough Institute

Established by Ted Nordhaus and Michael Shellenberger, the California-based Breakthrough Institute grew out of a provocative and widely disseminated essay released in 2004 under the title *The Death of Environmentalism*. Distributed at the annual meeting of the Environmental Grantmakers Association, an organization of large philanthropies that provides significant financial support to mainstream environmental groups, the authors set out from the start to shake up the stodgy world of charitable patronage. The authors' bombshell message was that environmentalism was little more than another special interest and the leadership of major organizations was mostly out of touch with the concerns of ordinary people. A central proposal was a call to launch a "New Apollo Project" which would be a two-year initiative to build a broad bipartisan coalition to support a national renewable energy program.

During the immediate aftermath of their essay, Shellenberger and Nordhaus traversed the United States and in some venues were greeted as lion slayers who had the temerity to take on the "environmental lobby," which at the time was having little success in challenging the regressive policies of the George W. Bush presidential administration. As expected, the proposition of forging alliances with age-old adversaries set off a firestorm; climate activist and author Bill McKibben famously branded them "the bad boys of environmentalism." Despite this acclaim, the message that Nordhaus and Shellenberger delivered was not necessarily new. Membership in most major environmental organizations had by that point been on a steady decline for more than a decade and they were not the first observers to issue a death certificate.

Nonetheless, extensive media attention generated by this episode enabled Nordhaus and Shellenberger to establish Breakthrough Institute in 2007. Since then, the Institute has been conducting research, advocating for proactive environmental technology policies, and providing consultancy services that stress technological solutions to environmental problems. It disavows initiatives predicated on regulation and target-setting in favor of strategies specifically designed to reduce the cost of clean energy and hence "reconcile the conflict between global economic development and climate mitigation."

The Breakthrough Institute came back into public prominence in 2015 with publication of an essay entitled *An Ecomodernist Manifesto* (Asatu-Adjaye et al. 20167). Based on the work of 18 authors, the statement renounces any claims to human harmony with nature and instead asserts that "intensifying many human activities – particularly farming, energy extraction, forestry, and settlement – so that they use less land and interfere less with the natural world is the key to decoupling human development from environmental impacts." The document further contends that planetary boundaries are "so theoretical as to be functionally irrelevant" and that human society can continue to flourish by relying on energy delivered through "a closed uranium or thorium fuel cycle, or from hydrogen-deuterium fusion." The authors are in no way convinced that constraints on land availability represent a threat to humanity's ability to feed ourselves.

Source: Nordhaus and Shellenberger (2005, 2007); Asatu-Adjaye, et al., *An Ecomodernist Manifesto.* Oakland, CA: Breakthrough Institute, 2016. Breakthrough Institute: https://thebreakthrough.org.

Ecological Modernization in Practice

A variety of technocentric approaches fit under the umbrella of ecological modernization. Several of these tools and strategies were outlined above and this section aims to highlight additional ways in which engineering techniques are currently being applied to reduce resource use, mitigate the effects of climate change, and more generally strive to enhance the sustainability of contemporary lifestyles and provisioning practices. It merits noting that references to the SDGs, because they devote prominent attention to poverty reduction and social inclusion, have what is oftentimes an ambivalent relationship with ecomodernist ideas. The following discussion considers three conceptual approaches: circular economy, biomimicry, and Earth system engineering and management. In addition, brief attention is devoted to two nascent policy programs – the Green New Deal and Industry 4.0.

Circular Economy

Current systems of production and consumption are primarily organized on a linear basis. This characterization means that raw materials are extracted, processed into components for assembly, fabricated into manufactured goods, distributed to consumers, and, finally, discarded as trash. In the case of some items – for example plastic water bottles or automobiles – a limited amount of recycling or reuse may occur, but, for the most part, we can describe the system as being predicated on the notion of "take-make-waste."

Because of the prodigious amount of waste associated with contemporary consumer lifestyles, we seek to exploit nonrenewable resources from evermore distant and inaccessible locales that create widening patterns of social and environmental disruption. The situation is also responsible for the massive accumulation of packaging materials, cast-off electronics, construction materials, and household garbage that we send to landfills or transport to incineration facilities (including to so-called "waste-to-energy" plants). In some parts of the world, significant volumes of trash end up floating down rivers, where the detritus piles up in coastal ecosystems or is carried by ocean currents to remote areas of the marine environment. The most famous and dramatic accumulation is the so-called Great Pacific Garbage Patch (GPGP), which was first observed in 1988 and presently contains an estimated 7 million tons of waste plastics (Lebreton et al. 2018).

Drawing heavily on principles of industrial ecology, the concept of a *circular economy* seeks to develop new modes of materials management that encourage expansive remanufacturing and recycling as well as facilitating product reuse and more cooperative arrangements for sharing consumer goods. The overall aim is to shift production and consumption away from linearity and ultimately achieve a closed system where resources are either continuously recirculated within the industrial system or become biological nutrients. While enhanced recycling is often regarded as a key strategy for a circular economy, required improvements are not achievable solely on the basis of conscientious action on the part of consumers and other end-users. Most goods at present are not designed and manufactured to enable effective recovery of materials, thus there is a need to reconsider how chemicals, textiles, machined components, and so forth are created during the earliest stages of their production processes. Moreover, prevalent commercial incentives purposefully encourage premature obsolescence, high turnover, and rapid discarding as a way to accelerate replacement and enhance sales.

Most proponents of a circular economy typically stress the importance of adopting new business models that emphasize the provision of services (so-called product-service systems or products of service) and the extension of product lifespans. Certain forms of employment – notably in the raw materials extraction sector – would be eliminated, but new jobs and economic opportunities would likely be created, enhancing the durability of consumer goods and integrating and maintaining the reliable flow of embedded services. A popular trend is the emergence of Internet-based companies (or platforms) that enable consumers to rent products for short periods of time rather than having to purchase them outright. This concept has been operationalized for the serial leasing of, for example, tools, textbooks, and bicycles (and other urban mobility technologies). A mode that has begun to achieve increasing appeal involves the rental of clothing and fashion accessories, which enables users to acquire stylish apparel at a fraction of the price that it would cost if bought outright.[3]

A particularly noteworthy recent effort to facilitate circularity in practice is a project called Loop conceived and implemented by the US-based company TerraCycle. The firm has recruited a sizable number of multinational companies including PepsiCo, Proctor & Gamble, and

Unilever to redesign their product packages using stainless steel or other durable materials. Consumers set up an account and then place an order via the Loop website. The items are delivered via parcel service in a specially designed tote bag. Packaging materials from products that have been consumed are returned when new supplies are dropped off. The empty containers are sorted at a Loop facility before being directed back to the manufacturer for refilling and redeployment. The aim is to create a (semi-) closed loop (or zero-waste) system for these materials, and recent reports suggest that the specially designed canisters can be used upwards of 100 times before they need to be replaced. In many respects, Loop is not a new idea but – by its own admission – a rediscovered concept that traces back to the system that was once in place in many communities for home delivery of milk in reusable glass bottles.

Earth system engineering and management

Proponents of Earth system engineering and management (ESEM) regard themselves, at least in metaphoric terms, as planetary firefighters. In other words, while one hopes never to need to call for emergency assistance, it is important to have capable and well-trained personnel on hand when disaster strikes. Such help is even more important when the occupants of a building have a tendency to play with flammable materials. The same goes for the planet.

Human beings are engaged in various dangerous activities – from toxifying the soil, to altering the albedo of the world through massive land-use changes, to injecting vast volumes of greenhouse gases into the atmosphere. We do not know when we will hit critical tipping points, but if these boundaries are transgressed, the future of humanity (and other living species) could be profoundly jeopardized. The field of ESEM seeks to develop the technologies and scientific interventions that could be activated in the case of a crisis. Indeed, the sense of urgency has increased in recent decades as the pace and extent of human interference with the Earth system has reached new proportions. Proponents of ESEM contend that failure to recognize the scope of our activities, or to think that we can make necessary and timely adaptations at different geographic scales, is a kind of delusional thinking. It is imperative to acknowledge that we have fundamentally, but poorly, redesigned the planet for our own purposes. Accordingly, there is no corner of the world – regardless of how pristine it may superficially seem – that has not been disrupted and reconfigured by human interference.

Instead of pulling back, we must, consistent with ecological modernization, develop the necessary scientific understanding and managerial expertise to more capably and rationally direct biospheric processes. We do not have the luxury of engaging in romantic or escapist thinking. Humanity has long manipulated the regenerative capacity of the Earth, mostly in haphazard and indiscriminate ways. ESEM contends that we must manifest a new civilizational maturity and take responsibility for our actions. This obligation entails acting purposefully and with a sense of stewardship to implement ameliorative remedies that reverse the damage as we increasingly become aware of the scale of the harm we have caused (and are continuing to cause).

While ESEM has, to date, been applied with some success in modest settings involving water management in places such as Florida and the Netherlands, it is with respect to climate change that it has received the most attention (in these instances, the terms geoengineering or climate engineering are frequently employed). With respect to greenhouse-gas removal (sometimes termed "negative emissions technologies"), possible interventions have ranged from large-scale planting of trees to carbon capture and storage schemes to widespread ocean dispersal of iron filings. In the case of the latter proposal, the idea is that the small pieces of iron would increase plankton growth and the organisms would absorb surplus carbon dioxide. As the plankton died and sank, the retained carbon dioxide would be sequestered on the bottom of the ocean.

Other commonly discussed concepts include technologies to deflect solar radiation away from the Earth and back out into space, thus serving to offset some of the effects of climate change. Specific ideas for so-called "sunshade geoengineering" include the construction and positioning of orbiting satellites with large mirrors, or the injection of reflective aerosols into the stratosphere. It is also worth mentioning the relatively modest strategies for achieving similar objectives that include, for example, installing white roofing materials on buildings or covering existing roofs with light-colored paint. Roof gardens can also be effective in ameliorating urban heat island effects – a concept that has proved quite popular in some communities.

Debates surrounding ESEM have become more fervent over the past decade or so as the need to consider active use of the more elaborate technologies has started to become less hypothetical. The Intergovernmental Panel on Climate Change (IPCC), as well as several national scientific councils, has begun to devote increasing attention to geoengineering in recent years. Aside from the ultimate workability and effectiveness of these schemes at a significant scale, critics have voiced concerns about their unintended consequences as well as their economic feasibility. For instance, the implementation of ESEM measures could displace the urgency to reduce greenhouse-gas emissions. In addition, although solar radiation management could potentially forestall rising global temperatures, it would have little positive effect on other aspects of atmospheric accumulation of carbon dioxide such as increasing ocean acidification.

Biomimicry

Biomimicry (or biomimetics) involves the evocative prospect of turning to nature for solutions to what are otherwise technological problems. Popularized by science writer Janine Benyus (1997), the general presumption underlying the field is that biological organisms have evolved capacities over millennia to overcome various obstacles that threatened their survival and reproductive potential. Researchers working in this field contend that we can learn from these processes of discovery and redirect the accumulated resourcefulness to meet human-scale challenges. For instance, biomimicry has been used to manufacture super-strong materials with the same properties as a spider web (five times stronger than steel), automobile tires that have wet adhesion capabilities similar to a tree frog, projectiles for use in water that are designed in the shape of a shark, and aircraft constructed to resemble the wings of a bird. Some researchers have sought to create engineered artifacts such as bridges and ships that have the ability to repair themselves when damaged or deteriorated using techniques found in abalone shells. A particularly renowned example of biomimicry involves the formulation of a paint that has similar self-cleaning properties as the leaves of lotus plants. Surfaces covered with the material remain dirt-free for as long as five years (Robbins 2001).

The sustainability implications of biomimicry derive from an under-standing that human-engineered technologies are unduly risky and uncertain because they have not been subjected to the same kinds of rigorous and lengthy testing that biological evolution has exerted on nonhuman species. By contrast, natural selection has tested bio-based solutions over long periods and less adequate techniques have gradually been supplanted by superior alternatives. The current state of evolu-tionary biology is a composite of historically proven answers that we can appropriate for contemporary purposes. Despite the extraordinary power of our own ingenuity, it is unlikely that we will be able to match the methods that have survived this long and arduous process of experimentation.

We can thus find in nature ideas that enable us to design energy-efficient buildings that incorporate the climate-control architecture used in termite hives, wind turbines that model the body shape of humpback whales, and high-speed trains that resemble kingfishers. However, it is important not to underestimate the conceptual obstacles of using biomimicry to inform design decisions and to go beyond a few novel applications. As Emily Kennedy and her colleagues at the Biomimicry Research and Innovation Center at the University of Akron observe, the sensibilities of the industrial design paradigm are deeply rooted and will not easily be superseded by biomimetic alternatives. The authors write: "Biomimicry does not necessarily render sustainable outcomes, and we cannot overlook this fact. A biomimetic solution could get high marks in functional performance but fail miserably in a sustainable life cycle analysis" (2015: 69).

Green New Deal

The Green New Deal (GND) was first articulated as a political manifesto and then variously incorporated into policy programs and legislative proposals in several different countries. The concept draws inspiration both rhetorically and substantively from the original New Deal launched during the 1930s by former US President Franklin Delano Roosevelt, and comprised a vast array of programs to catalyze sweeping social and economic reforms. Analysts assign credit for "greening" the New Deal to the *New York Times* columnist Thomas Friedman (2007), who used the term in an opinion article to describe a far-reaching plan for environmentally led social investment and policy reform. Central to the proposal was abolition of subsidies on fossil fuels while instituting a carbon tax, and creating a durable scheme to scale up the production of renewable energy.

As detailed by journalist Alexander Kaufman (2018), the idea was then picked up by presidential candidate Barack Obama to describe a proposed package of economic stimulus measures after the 2008 financial crisis. The concept then diffused globally. The London-based New Economics Foundation (NEF) initially popularized the concept in the United Kingdom and it subsequently received support from grassroots groups in the country as well as leading figures in the Labour Party, which held power at the time (Green New Deal Group 2008; Simms 2009). The UNEP also released a report entitled *The Global Green New Deal* (Barbier 2010).

After this initially successful wave, the US House of Representatives passed a version of GND legislation called the American Clean Energy and Security Act of 2009, but the Senate never took it up. The UK government established a public bank to spur investment in green technologies consistent with GND thinking, but then it was declared that there was no money available to pay for such an ambitious program.

Aside from a scattering of articles in academic journals and writings by sympathetic eco-socialist authors, the notion of a GND had mostly disappeared by 2010. It was not until almost a decade later that the idea resurfaced, first during the 2016 presidential campaign of US Senator Bernie Sanders and then as part of the insurgent candidacy of his protégé Alexandria Ocasio-Cortez, who successfully ran as a social democrat for a congressional seat representing a working-class district of New York City. In its reincarnated form, a GND built around a carbon tax was more decisively married to a plan calling for substantial infrastructure investment, technological innovation, and creation of new employment opportunities building a green economy. Other progressive Democrats in the country endorsed the essential outlines of a GND, and in 2019 Congresswoman Ocasio-Cortez released, with significant grassroots support, a resolution (H. Res 109) asserting that it was "the duty of the Federal Government to create a Green New Deal."

The proposal – which is more a declaration of intent than a fully developed legislative document – recognizes that human activity is the most prominent contributing cause of climate change, and that accumulation of greenhouse-gas emissions is responsible for impacts ranging from sea-level rise, increasingly destructive wildfires and extreme weather, mass migration, and property damage. The resolution calls for reducing climate-altering pollution by 40–60 percent from 2010 levels by 2030 and for achieving "net-zero global emissions by 2050." As envisioned, a GND aims to achieve a fair and just transition for all communities and workers, to create millions of high-wage jobs, and to invest in infrastructure and industry to enhance national competitiveness. In addition, it strives to secure availability of clean air and water, to build the climate resiliency of communities, to enhance provision of healthy food, and to ensure access to nature and a sustainable environment. Similar propositions have recently been advanced in the United Kingdom and other countries and regions (Pettifor 2019; Adler 2019), suggesting that the GND has decidedly gathered a second wind, though it is unlikely to move to the center of policy agendas in the absence of enabling processes of political change.

In both letter and spirit, the GND is avowedly committed to robust economic growth achieved through substantial public investment and reliance on new technologies (see also Rifkin 2019). The envisioned transition is broadly consistent with the tenets of ecological modernization and premised on a hopeful and implicit expectation that, by renewing strategic elements of the technological infrastructure, we can decouple economic growth from resource utilization. Despite the outsized scale of the challenge, current expressions of this political program are notable from an ecomodernist vantage point for the attention that they devote to enhancing societal well-being, improving economic security, and reducing poverty.

Industry 4.0

Human civilization has advanced through three successive waves of momentous sociotechnical change (see Chapter 2). The first significant shift occurred approximately 10,000 years ago and involved a transition from migratory foraging to more settled agriculture. This agrarian revolution was followed by the first industrial revolution, which initially gathered momentum during the second half of the eighteenth century, and, as earlier discussed, was powered by widespread deployment of the steam engine and associated production technologies. It was subsequently further enabled in a second phase by advent of the railroad and electricity, which catalyzed development of the assembly line. Computerization and the eventual arrival of the Internet impelled a third wave of industrial transformation.

Economists of technological change have formulated various chronological schemes that share a number of similarities with this common historical framework. During the 1920s, the Russian economist Nikolai Kondratiev (2014 [1935]), observed that there had been, since the mid-eighteenth century, several successive waves (or long cycles) of innovation, which had unfolded in a consistent and reliable pattern. This idea was more widely promoted a decade later by Austrian political economist Joseph Schumpeter (1961), who coined the term "creative destruction." As shown in Figure 3.1, this regularized process of technological evolution entailed the advent of the steam engine and dramatic improvements in textile production (1785–1845), the mass production of steel and the construction of railways (1845–1900), the emergence of electrical engineering and chemistry (1900–1950), the rise of petrochemicals and automobiles (1950–1990), and the development of digital networks and associated applications (1990–Present).

Regardless of how we segment the arc of technological change, the claim made by more recent proponents of this general line of thinking is that a new wave of ingenuity is about to unfold. First formulated by German engineer and social entrepreneur Klaus Schwab (2016a), the claim is that "[w]e stand on the brink of a technological revolution that will fundamentally alter the way we live, work, and relate to one another. In its scale, scope, and complexity, the transformation will be unlike anything humankind has experienced before." This period will be predicated on a new generation of innovation that "[blurs] the lines between the physical, digital, and biological spheres" (Schwab

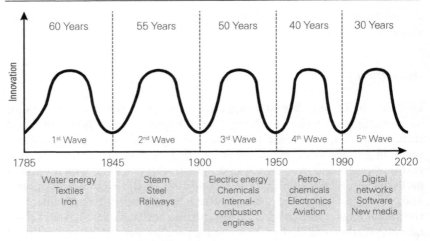

Figure 3.1   Schumpeter's waves of creative destruction

Source: Based on Figure 1 in Milica Jovanovic, Jasmina Dlacic, and Milan Okanovic, Digitalization and society's sustainable development: Measures and implications, *Proceedings of Rijeka School of Economics* 36(2), 2018: 905–928.

2016b). It will be an era that is simultaneously characterized by social disruption and human advancement. At the heart of this upheaval will be several interlinked cyberphysical technologies, including implantable mobile phones, Internet of Things, smart homes and cities, autonomous vehicles, robotics, artificial intelligence, and much more.

A so-called Fourth Industrial Revolution will extend far beyond what we customarily construe as issues most directly pertinent to sustainability. As Schwab (2016b) asserts:

> Already, artificial intelligence is all around us, from self-driving cars and drones to virtual assistants and software that translate or invest. Impressive progress has been made in AI in recent years, driven by exponential increases in computing power and by the availability of vast amounts of data, from software used to discover new drugs to algorithms used to predict our cultural interests. Digital fabrication technologies, meanwhile, are interacting with the biological world on a daily basis. Engineers, designers, and architects are combining computational design, additive manufacturing, materials engineering, and synthetic biology to pioneer a symbiosis between microorganisms, our bodies, the products we consume, and even the buildings we inhabit.

Yet even the most ardent champions of the Fourth Industrial Revolution recognize that the forthcoming challenges are great, and not just in terms of ensuring a steady flow of commercially feasible technological breakthroughs. Ample evidence suggests the prosperity generated by innovation tends to accrue to individuals with the most intellectual talent and financial capital. In a world already riven by widening income and wealth inequalities, and the political polarization that these trends have already engendered, a period of accelerating technology-driven social change holds the prospect for very serious turmoil.

In addition, the technologies at the heart of this emergent revolution have the capacity to collect vast amounts of data and to empower governments and others to develop extraordinary powers of surveillance. The consequences of these developments are already apparent, even at this relatively early stage of transformation. Privacy is under threat and it remains unclear whether capacity to ensure adequate protection will become effective features of these technologies. There is furthermore the prospect that our very humanity is apt to evolve in new directions as we increasingly merge with our devices (Bostrom 2016). The boundaries between our biology and our technology will become blurrier as artificial intelligence and physical augmentation become more widespread and capable. The effects of such developments with respect to sustainability are likely to be substantial and will probably be difficult to anticipate with any precision from contemporary vantage points. While the hope is that the benefits of this wave of innovation will enhance the prosperity of people in greatest need, there is deep uncertainty as to how we can effectively assure this outcome given weak governance at both local and global levels.

Can the Engineers Deliver a Sustainable Future?

Late in 2015, representatives from more than 200 countries met in France to complete final negotiations on a landmark international accord to address climate change. Legally part of the UNFCCC discussed in Chapter 1, the so-called Paris Agreement requires signatory governments to develop a plan to reduce their releases of carbon dioxide and other heat-trapping gases and to regularly report on progress meeting the established targets. The overall goal of the agreement is to prevent average global temperatures from exceeding 2°C above pre-industrial levels and to strive for more ambitious reductions to limit the increase to 1.5°C. This undertaking is generally regarded as requiring a reduction of 80 percent below 1990 levels by 2050 (Rogelj et al. 2016).

Building on the MDGs outlined in Table 1.1, the United Nations has separately facilitated in recent years an international process to formulate an expansive array of 17 sustainable development goals, which center on achieving explicit humanitarian objectives ranging from ending hunger to providing quality education to fostering sustainable production and consumption by 2030.

With respect to both the climate target and the SDG objectives, time is extremely short, and we clearly need to get moving if we are going to have any chance of success. These commitments place enormous pressure on industrial ecologists, ecological designers, Earth system engineers, and other practitioners of ecological modernization to set the planet on a new path. A question with profound consequences is whether we should put the fate of humanity and the rest of the biosphere in their hands, however confident and assuring their pronouncements might be. The dilemma that we face is that, if technocentric strategies are not going to be sufficient, we will need to start looking elsewhere for other interventions or perhaps even an entirely different approach that offers better odds.

It is essential to acknowledge that engineering our way to sustainability offers some important advantages and we should not prematurely abandon this alternative. It is necessary to acknowledge that we live in a world where democratic values are regularly being undermined, economic opportunities are allocated based on existing privilege, inequality is deeply endemic, and the public seems to be at best weakly cognizant of the global challenges that we all face (Levitsky and Ziblatt 2018; Acemoglu and Robinson 2019). Such circumstances suggest that it may not be unreasonable to count on the capabilities of the technologists. After all, where else can we turn?

Moreover, the engineers are not shy when it comes to vision. Plans to encase the Earth in sunshields or to rebuild the world's megacities using smart-city architectures are nothing if not audacious.[4] These ecomodernist aspirations may not find universal appeal, but the current state of urgency may preclude us from indulging in diversionary debates about how to design more dialogic policy processes or to encourage sustainable behavior on a rapidly warming planet that will soon have more than 8 billion mostly poor people (Laurent 2013).

It therefore comes down to whether we can confidently count on ecological modernization and its associated modes of practical application to achieve the necessary transformations. There are important reasons why we should be circumspect. While environmental science and engineering have contributed to significant improvements in a number of key areas, these gains have typically been accompanied by concomitant social changes and other adaptive responses. For example, the air in cities (at least in wealthier countries) is cleaner today because of the implementation of advanced environmental technologies (such as catalytic converters on cars and pollution-control devices on electric-utility plants), but a concurrent driver has been the exportation of industrial production to low-cost production sites around the world. Moreover, engineering-informed strategies to manage environmental hazards due to, for instance, flooding and extreme weather have tended to exacerbate problems. Generally, the implementation of technology displaces problems geographically or temporally instead of resolving them in any comprehensive sense. There may be an illusion of improvement in a particular locale or timeframe, but that is only because the dilemma has been supplanted from one place to another or pushed out into the future.[5] Social critic Evgeny Morozov (2014) has termed this phenomenon "technological solutionism."

There are, though, other reasons why we need to exercise care and avoid uncritically and prematurely embracing technological options or regarding them as the only way forward. The engineering paradigm is heavily oriented toward seeking improvements in efficiency (or eco-efficiency in the language of sustainability) and a long history has shaped this priority. Dating back at least as far as the mid-nineteenth century and the insights of the British economist William Stanley Jevons (1865), analysts have recognized that gains in efficiency are apt to lead to increases instead of decreases in aggregate consumption. Jevons's primary point of concern was the relationship between the steam engine and the consumption of coal. Mechanical engineers of the day demonstrated ruthless commitment to enhancing the efficiency of this Victorian-era machine, which, as described earlier in this chapter, played such a critical role in industrialization. The predicament, and the shrewdness of Jevons's understanding, was that improvements in technical efficiency had the effect of driving down operational costs and expanding the use of steam engines. Ultimately, during this period coal consumption increased markedly as new uses for the fuel multiplied with each passing year.

Importantly, this is not just an industrial-age anomaly. Numerous, more recent examples abound. The implementation of automotive fuel-economy standards in the United States during the 1970s reduced the per-mile cost of driving and encouraged people to drive longer distances and to purchase larger cars. The result was that, on a national basis, gasoline consumption increased. Significant improvements in the energy efficiency of household refrigerators (as measured on a cubic unit basis) prompted consumers to upgrade to larger appliances.[6] Similar perverse effects occurred with respect to air conditioning (installation of cooling units in rooms that had been left warm under prior circumstances) and lighting (more efficient illumination led to the placement of bulbs in places that were previously left in nighttime darkness) (Cox 2010).

A common rebuttal is that the untoward outcomes in these cases are not the result of ill-conceived engineering, but regrettably stem from the fact that users acted in unexpected and ill-advised ways. In other words, the innovations were correctly conceived and deployed. The problems started after consumers put the technologies into service. The accuracy of this interpretation is debatable, but we do not need to parse the claim here.[7] Assigning blame to imprudent drivers and homeowners misses the point. The fact that the new systems do not work in the real world, regardless of the cause, is a design failure. Neglecting to include the routines of users of more ostensibly energy-efficient automobiles and appliances means that the engineers misconceived their assignment. People (along with their messy and sometimes irascible practices), as well as larger processes of social and economic change, cannot simply be airbrushed out of the design brief because such issues pose inconvenient complications. Virtually all technologies – from coffee makers to solar panels – are simultaneously and inseparably social and technical systems and it is a fatal mistake to cut ordinary people out of the equation or to ascribe responsibility to them when actual performance does not align with expectations.

Engineer and sustainability scientist Michael Huesemann (2003) develops this argument further when he asks why seemingly proficient experts are unable to anticipate the consequences of technology.[8] Consistent with the parable discussed in Chapter 2 about the blind men and the elephant, Huesemann attributes the predicament to limitations in the scientific method, which relies on reductionism – breaking problems into more readily solvable parts. Under certain circumstances, this approach can be extraordinarily powerful and, indeed, it unquestionably has led to many important insights. However, the drawback is that by looking only at a manageable number of variables in isolation, the scientific method loses sight of the larger picture. When we put our faith in powerful technologies based on fragmentary knowledge of their potential impacts on the whole system, we end up generating unfortunate, and occasionally calamitous, outcomes. These fateful situations include species extinction, climate change, soil toxicity, and air and water pollution. Once problems become apparent, the standard response, as Huesemann and others contend, is to apply another layer of technology rather than committing ourselves to identifying root causes.

Conclusion

Historical experience suggests that we need to temper our confidence and adopt a generally skeptical posture when evaluating the promise of technology-led sustainability strategies. It is not that the engineers who carry out this work lack valor or rectitude. It is often quite the opposite. The challenge instead is that technological systems are not separate and apart from the wider world – they are fundamentally sociotechnical systems and, in the broad sense, are neither inherently sustainable nor unsustainable. The specific features of their performance are determined by the social and political context in which they are deployed and this is a matter about which this book will have more to say in the chapters that follow.

In the meantime, it is important to keep in mind the observation made by pioneering environmental scientist Donella Meadows (2008), specifically that we must be certain that our technologies are oriented in the correct direction. This principle is violated more frequently than we are typically prepared to acknowledge. The prevailing practice is to launch innovations into the world – sometimes with a veneer of sustainability – to increase the value of stock portfolios, to ensure a company's competitive advantage, to elevate national prestige, and other similar motivations. Under such circumstances, it is almost inevitable that these technologies will give rise to adverse consequences and other unintended outcomes. The lesson here is that we need to learn to conceive of sustainability within the context of whole systems. This does not mean that we should dispense completely with reductionism, but rather that customary techniques ought to be balanced with a broader conception of how our innovations will interact with society and the world at large.

Given the large breach that exists between technical expertise and comprehension of the wider context, forging joined-up thinking is oftentimes not an easy undertaking. Fortunately, useful progress is being made to create frameworks that engage different communities of practice in the search for more comprehensive conceptual understanding. Commitment to this mode of knowledge acquisition relies on new forms of experimentation that transcend the isolated trials that take place in laboratories and design studios under controlled conditions. A particularly interesting approach entails development of "post-normal" technologies through expansive stakeholder engagement and coproduction of knowledge involving extended peer communities comprising technical and tacit knowledge. A related concept involves both experts and nonexperts in creation of so-called "living labs" that provide a user-centric setting based on open innovation to allow researchers and other project participants to test emergent ideas and applications in real-world settings. The emphasis is on co-creation and joint exploration to foster experiential learning. First launched at MIT in 2011, the concept has spread to a number of universities and other institutions in Europe, Asia, and elsewhere around the world. Particularly valuable in recent years has been the establishment of living labs that encourage realistic experimentation with technologies and novel social practices intended to foster sustainable living.

4

Planning Sustainability Transitions

Introduction

Sustainability scientists and engineers have been contributing to ongoing efforts to identify opportunities to decouple economic growth from resource utilization and we need to leverage their insights to the fullest extent possible. However, there are compelling reasons to presume that this work, important though it is, will ultimately be inadequate to keep global temperature rises from exceeding 1.5°C, reverse the pace of biodiversity losses, reduce global inequality, or make progress on the SDGs. A sustainable future is also predicated on reinventing political institutions, social practices, and cultural norms. Because of the formidable obstacles that stand in the way of change in these domains, there has been an understandable tendency to sidestep the associated challenges. Instead, the prevailing emphasis has been to seek technological pathways and to hope that the necessary breakthroughs will occur in a timely manner.

Debates about whether humanity has crossed the threshold into the Anthropocene are another feature of the current era and are likely to continue. At the same time, we should not lose sight of the fact that nearly three centuries of industrialization have already altered the Earth system in profound and probably irreversible ways. While the notion of planetary boundaries has been vitally important to contemporary understanding, the most compelling issue is not whether we are on the edge of overwhelming biogeochemical processes. As geographer Erle Ellis (2018) instructively contends, "[t]he real question is how we better negotiate among ourselves, across all our many diverse peoples and cultures, also that we can navigate together toward the better futures we wish for, in our different ways."

Focusing primarily on affluent countries, this chapter first looks at how we might embark on this process, which will require making significant adjustments in the complex organizational arrangements that enable and maintain contemporary lifestyles. Second, the discussion considers conceptual developments at the nexus of innovation studies, science and technology studies, and the history and sociology of technology. Researchers in these fields have formulated a widely used analytic framework for studying prospective sustainability transitions known as the Multi-Level Perspective (MLP). Third, several other methodological approaches are highlighted that have been applied to envisage transformational modes of system innovation. Fourth, consideration is devoted to the important role of cities as critical geographic nodes for shifts toward more sustainable sociotechnical systems. Fifth, the discussion focuses attention on the emergent notion of so-called Deep Transitions, which provide an historically informed interpretation of the prospect of systemic change. The chapter concludes by reflecting on how these conceptual frameworks might contribute to efforts to forge more sustainable systems of consumption and production.

Enhancing the Sustainability of Consumption and Production

Both explicit and crosscutting challenges of the SDGs include how to achieve more environmentally tenable and socially equitable allocations of the materials and energy devoted to consumption and production.[1] This section introduces four overlapping concepts that have shaped current understanding of how to enhance the environmental and social performance of contemporary provisioning practices: sociotechnical systems, system innovations, sustainability transitions, and transition management.

To begin, it merits observing that the past few decades have been characterized by a widespread tendency to venerate individualism and self-made achievement, while simultaneously maintaining an overly simplified understanding of technology. Though the observation challenges popular dogma, we are not so much the architects of our own lives as we are actors embedded in and enabled by expansive technological configurations. These systems are partly social and partly technical and hence it is common to refer to them as *sociotechnical systems*. On the one hand, the social dimensions include regulations, consumer preferences and expectations, knowledge, norms, and cultural dispositions. On the other, the technical elements comprise automobiles, electric utility power plants, factories, warehouses, highways, and much more. Especially critical sociotechnical systems from the standpoint of sustainability are the surface-transportation system, the energy-supply system, the water-delivery system, the agro-food system, the educational system, and the healthcare system.

Because they are common and everyday features of our lives, we normally do not think much about sociotechnical systems and the details of their maintenance and ongoing operation. When walking up and down the aisles of the supermarket, we rarely reflect on the complex combinations of human labor and technology that are required to put food on the shelves. Similarly, while driving to work we would likely be overwhelmed if we had to account for the multitudes of people and devices necessary to ensure that the roadways are in functional form. By contrast, we become more attentive to sociotechnical systems when they show signs of distress or collapse altogether, as is sometimes the case in the wake of major natural disasters. During ordinary times, however, they function more or less satisfactorily and we mostly take them for granted. Unfortunately, concerns about sustainability have not had, at least to date, much influence on the design of prevalent sociotechnical systems. Other objectives have instead been paramount, including assuring profitability, elevating national prestige, ensuring employment creation, raising personal incomes, and narrowing inter-regional disparities.

The objective for sustainability proponents is how to transition from contemporary sociotechnical systems that all too often undermine human well-being and environmental integrity of the Earth system to alternatives that are consistent with these goals. This is an extremely difficult undertaking and brings to mind the metaphor about trying to repair an airplane while it is in flight. Because sociotechnical systems provide goods and services on which we depend – mobility, energy, food, and so forth – we typically do have the ability to shut down currently operating modes while deploying improved replacements.

This brings us to the second key concept. It is becoming increasingly apparent that climate change and other sustainability challenges are not amenable to customary technological-fix solutions. Instead, the complexity and scale of these problems demand more robust and far-reaching social changes, especially with respect to societal institutions and governance. Researchers and practitioners refer to such transformations as *system innovations* (Elzen et al. 2004; Geels 2005). According to the Organisation for Economic Co-operation and Development (OECD 2016):

> [S]ystem innovation is motivated by the realization that system-wide changes are necessary to make economies socially, economically and environmentally sustainable. Although many national governments have put sustainability and green growth objectives at the centre of their economic development strategies, achieving this goal will require wide-ranging changes in their underlying economic, technological, and social systems, from transport, water and energy systems to modes of consumption and waste management. Ensuring that socio-technical systems move towards greater sustainability is a major challenge for governments but also for civil society.

Consistent with the discussion above, system innovations have both social and technical components and these two facets can coevolve to produce disruptive transformations that differ dramatically from more familiar processes of incremental change that occur in terms of, for example, improvements in the energy efficiency of household appliances. These types of relatively modest adjustment can normally be accommodated by the existing sociotechnical system and have little or no impact on the wider technological configuration or the social arrangements in which they are embedded. For instance, the experience of purchasing a car with a higher fuel-economy rating is little different from what one would encounter if buying a vehicle that did not have this feature. The two automobiles would utilize the same infrastructure, be subject to the same regulations, and require the same skills to operate. Under such circumstances, there is also the prospect of rebound effects as the new car would have lower operating costs and, as discussed in Chapter 3, trigger the likelihood of more rather than less driving.

So what kind of change needs to be catalyzed for it to be regarded as a system innovation? A transformation of this scale would entail the implementation of a new business model, the deployment of a radically different technology, or the advent of novel user practices (or all three of these changes). It furthermore might take several years (or decades) for all the necessary social and technical elements to converge into a practicable and cost-effective configuration (McMeekin et al. 2019). Furthermore, the overall process, what we will refer to as a *sustainability transition*, is not likely to proceed along a continuous and linear trajectory, but rather entail a few initial steps followed by a period of stagnation, and then a subsequent phase of technical refinement and adoption by users. An example is a shift from centralized electricity generation based on combustion of coal to decentralized, community-based provision involving renewable sources of energy (see Box 4.1).

Box 4.1: Community energy

A growing number of communities in Germany, the Netherlands, the United Kingdom and elsewhere around the world are creating their own sources of electric-power generation based on wind, solar, or cogeneration biogas digesters. These arrangements allow residents to enhance their local resilience and to avoid having to purchase energy from large – often investor-owned – utility companies that tend to be indifferent and mostly unresponsive to public concerns about continued use of fossil-fuels and climate change. The creation of common and decentralized generating capacity also eliminates the need for individual households to install and manage their own renewable energy equipment. The underlying business model is generally a cooperative or municipal ownership.

Several contemporary community energy initiatives have grown out of grassroots-planning efforts undertaken by so-called Transition Towns, beginning in 2006, which have sought to foster energy autonomy and to facilitate low-carbon transitions by creating alternative supply networks. In some countries, governments have come to support these efforts through the provision of subsidies, tax incentives, and other measures. More than 200 community energy schemes operate in the United Kingdom and some of them reinvest their profits to construct recreation facilities and other projects that enhance the quality of life of local residents.

An example of a successful local energy provider is the Westmill Solar Cooperative in the United Kingdom, which describes itself as the world's largest cooperatively operated and community-owned solar farm. The 30-acre facility is located near Oxford and owned by its 1,500 members. It annually generates enough electricity to serve approximately 1,600 homes and prevents the annual emission of 2,000 tons of carbon dioxide.

Source: Gordon Walker and Neil Simcock, Community energy systems, pp. 194–198 in Susan Smith, ed., *International Encyclopedia of Housing and Home*. Amsterdam: Elsevier, 2012. Sylvia Pfeifer, Community energy projects bring power to the people, *Financial Times*, May 27, 2018: https://www.ft.com/content/c283a8a0-5f5e-11e8-9334-2218e7146b04. Westmill Solar Cooperative: http://westmillsolar.coop.

Box 4.2: Communal kitchens

Especially among feminist pioneers who sought during the early twentieth century to implement collectivized strategies for sharing household responsibilities, communal kitchens are a venerated and longstanding concept. The idea has resurfaced in recent years in a variety of forms and it is useful to distinguish between human rights canteens, collective kitchens, and community kitchens.

First, numerous local groups are part of an international network of *human rights canteens* that operate under the umbrella of *Food Not Bombs*. A group of antinuclear activists in Cambridge, Massachusetts, established the original organization in 1980. Some of its affiliates today continue a tradition of collecting unsold and discarded food, cooking and preparing the recovered supplies, and serving meals in public settings. Others provide meals to people engaged in protracted protests against injustice or deliver food aid in the aftermath of major natural disasters. For instance, local affiliates provided meals to volunteers after the attacks against the World Trade Center in New York City on September 11, 2001, and during the weeks following Hurricane Katrina in New Orleans in 2005.

Second, *collective kitchens* are organized by groups of people who pool their resources and come together to prepare communal and nutritious meals as part of routines to purchase food in bulk, to save money, to address food insecurity, to break down barriers to social isolation, and to build solidarity. These collaborations have become especially widespread in Canada with more than 1,000 such kitchens operating just in the province of Québec.

Finally, *community kitchens* are venues that provide opportunities for culinary education and cultural education. Meals are typically prepared by immigrant women with extensive experience cooking for their families, and the community kitchens enable them to share more broadly their knowledge of authentic ethnic cuisine. Participants pay a modest fee for the experience and the money enables the self-taught chefs to gain access to an important source of income.

Source: Food Not Bombs: http://foodnotbombs.net; Community Food Services Canada: https://cfccanada.ca/en/Home. "Community Kitchens" in *The Citizen's Handbook*: http://www.citizenshandbook.org/2_03_comm_kitchens.html.

Another instance of a prospective sustainability transition involves the development of urban networks to facilitate the shared cultivation, preparation, and distribution of food as this would mark a major departure from the currently predominant system in high-income countries based on market transactions (see Box 4.2).

Among sustainability researchers, there exists a lively debate concerning the extent to which sustainability transitions can be pursued in accordance with a comprehensive blueprint. On the one hand, advocates of *transition management* contend that, through planning and controlled experimentation, it is possible to develop shared visions of sociotechnical change and to steer unfolding processes along predetermined pathways. On the other hand, there is the view that transitions are inherently messy propositions, contingent on all sorts of unknown (and unknowable) variables, as well as shifting and conflictual politics.

The competing perspectives derive from the fact that countries have different capacities for administering and governing processes of innovation. This variation can be attributed to the persistence of distinct national innovation systems or national styles of innovation (Nelson 1993; Furman et al. 2002). For example, the Netherlands has an established tradition of industrial policy planning and a political culture that encourages consensus-oriented decision-making, both important capabilities when engaging in long-term term projects that require the participation and collaboration of a diverse array of societal stakeholders. Accordingly, the Dutch have embraced a relatively coordinated approach to system innovation and the pursuit of sustainability transitions in several industrial sectors. A roughly similar disposition to transition management is discernible, albeit to differing degrees, across most of Northern Europe. By contrast, the Anglospheric nations are less inclined to embrace the kind of centralized coordination and governmental control that is generally regarded as a precondition of transition management. The public sector typically plays a more circumscribed role in targeting research and development in these countries and is less likely to establish national priorities for system innovation or to engage in the development of policy plans for this purpose.

Multi-Level Perspective

Formulated at the interface of several interdisciplinary fields, including innovation studies, science and technology studies, and the history and sociology of technology, the MLP has become since the late 1990s an especially popular framework for studying sociotechnical transitions. A key figure in the advancement of the MLP has been Frank Geels, and researchers have used it to investigate cases ranging from low-carbon energy systems to sustainable agro-food systems to alternative transportation systems.

Explanation of the MLP begins by denoting the existence of three distinct tiers of analysis: a macro-level known as the *landscape*, a meso-level referred to as the *regime*, and a micro-level termed the *niches*. First, the landscape comprises the structural parameters – cultural norms, macroeconomic conditions, demographic characteristics, geopolitical relationships, and environmental and climatic parameters – of society that under normal circumstances is relatively invariable and immutable. We can conceive of the landscape in geological terms in the sense that it is sturdy and durable and endures over time with only gradual modification. When change occurs, it tends to transpire slowly and, generally, attentive observers can anticipate its pace and direction. However, consistent with the topographical comparison, occasionally unexpected seismic events (so-called "landscape shocks") can create pronounced and dramatic movement.

Second, the regime in the MLP comprises assemblages of institutions and other organizations that, in combination with particular sets of rules and routines, constitute an existing sociotechnical system. These are the companies, regulatory agencies, infrastructures, practices, standards, and so forth that have coevolved, typically over an extended period, and forged relationships of mutual reliance and systemic coordination. Their linkages are secured through a combination of legal, transactional, political, and social commitments, with the result being that these are not simply casual associations but, rather, relationships based on both formal and informal modes of codependency.

It is through these interlocking arrangements that the complexity of everyday life is created and reproduced. In tangible terms, the regime provides the multitude of goods and services on which society relies – oil, agricultural produce, automobiles, buildings, and much more. The performance of a regime (especially in terms of its sustainability) may be unsatisfactory in many respects. For instance, housing may be poorly insulated and overpriced, but it still provides people with shelter; food may be treated with chemical contaminants, but consumers are not undernourished; and fossil fuels may be the primary source of energy, but the most disruptive effects of climate change are still to be realized.

Finally, the micro-level of the MLP is the tier of the so-called niches. This is an extremely dynamic space characterized by vibrant innovation undertaken by future-oriented entrepreneurs. The niches ideally afford some measure of protection from competitive pressures and these conditions provide opportunity for initial growth. While this realm serves as the seedbed for new ideas and techniques, most of them will not see the light of day. This niche-based activity struggles to obtain financial resources and often lacks adequate managerial expertise to bring novel concepts to a scale where they could garner necessary support to achieve a level of stable growth. Part of the challenge is that prototypes conceived in the niches tend to be only partly compatible with the extant regime and are generally, in economic historian Joel Mokyr's (1990) colorful phase, "hopeful monstrosities." What is notable, though, is that occasionally an innovation attracts an effective team, secures funding, develops a solid marketing plan, recruits an initial customer base, and so forth. The inventive concept may also begin to align with other startups. Under these circumstances, it becomes possible to leverage the respective capabilities of the niche actors and to scale operations to a level that allows for a preliminary phase of organizational stability.

Initially successful innovations (or clusters of them) begin over time to gain visibility and to shed the relative obscurity of their niche. At this stage, the novel ideas will come into contact with the established institutions, organizations, and rules that comprise the regime. This interface between niche and regime is a particularly interesting feature of the MLP because this is where competition (and perhaps cooperation) occurs between insurgents and incumbents in the relevant sociotechnical system. In certain cases, regime actors will seek to undermine the vitality of the incipient innovation through strategic deployment of financial resources, marketing strategies, regulatory influence, or other capabilities. Additional responses might involve a regime actor in acquiring the relevant intellectual property and either pre-emptively retiring the innovation or harnessing it to its own business model.

It is also possible that, due to structural weakness or other incapacities within the dominant sociotechnical regime, a fortified niche-based innovation is able to successfully challenge and, under certain especially fortuitous conditions, supplant the incumbent arrangements. This process of transformation is likely to be further facilitated by timely accumulation of gradual changes – say in terms of demographic or cultural shifts that favor the innovation – at the level of the landscape. These circumstances would culminate in a successful transition as the former insurgent is installed as the new sociotechnical regime. At this point, a new iteration of competition between regime- and niche-based activities would commence.

A conceptual model such as the MLP is only useful to the extent that users deem it to provide an effective way to understand the complex and oftentimes obscure activities that surround processes of sociotechnical innovation. In the first instance, researchers have instructively applied the framework to a large number of historical cases. The most famous and iconic application of the MLP documents the process of cumulating change that led during the nineteenth century to the displacement of sailing ships by steamships (Geels 2002). Other case studies have focused on the shift to organic production in agricultural supply chains, the development of sanitary systems of water supply, the deployment of battery-electric vehicles, and the diffusion of ground-source heat-pump systems. The MLP has also been used to assess aborted or delayed transitions such as the failed effort (at least to date) to achieve less environmentally problematic modes of air travel and to implement a wind-powered offshore electric grid in the North Sea.

This work has helped to shed important light on processes of sociotechnical innovation. We know today a great deal more about the evolution of important transformations, but it is necessary to acknowledge that the framework has been primarily useful to organize retrospective studies of transitions and, as such, has been mostly valuable from a historical perspective. While past events can offer instructive guidance for prospective developments, the contingencies that inevitably characterize specific processes of system innovation have limited the ability of the MLP to inform prospective sociotechnical transitions. Efforts to study sustainable futures – or the history of the future, as some commentators have framed the undertaking – require different approaches, which are discussed in the next section.

Anticipating and Preparing for a Sustainable Future

As described in earlier chapters, the operationalizing of sustainability is heavily focused on quantitative metrics, efficiency improvements, and deployment of new technologies. An unfortunate consequence of this emphasis is that visions – a larger conception of how we might live in the future – tend to be pushed aside by technocentric analyses. Researchers have embraced the MLP, but this framework is arguably more useful for reconstructing the progression of prior sociotechnical innovations; its effectiveness in anticipating prospective developments is less apparent. This section describes three techniques that respond to the challenge of trying to comprehend how more sustainable futures might unfold: scenario analysis, future visioning, and backcasting.[2]

First, *scenario analysis*, especially in the context of military affairs, has a long been used to study the future. The advent of contemporary methodologies can be traced to the oil shocks of the 1970s when major industrial companies began to use scenarios to assess highly contingent business risks due to shifting macroeconomic and geopolitical factors (Schwartz 1991). Scenario analysis involves the identification of key drivers of future possibilities and assessment based on available and anticipated information concerning how they might combine to influence the likelihood of different alternatives. The aim is not to give preference to one particular outcome but, rather, to elaborate each option regardless of its presumed desirability. It merits observing that it can be extremely difficult to achieve this objective due to inevitable predispositions and biases on the part of the analysts.

Scenario analysis does not involve extrapolation of recent or existing tendencies, but seeks to identify plausible perturbations and to envisage how they might cause disruptions or discontinuities. The aim is to challenge analysts to work through the synergistic consequences that anticipated secondary and tertiary effects might have on strategic options, resources, organizational capabilities, and so forth. It is common for the results of such work to include pessimistic, optimistic, and so-called "business-as-usual" alternatives and then to use these scenarios to stimulate further consideration by relevant decision-makers. The primary advantage of the technique is to create "what if?" situations that motivate thought experiments and test organizational proficiencies for responding to low probability/high consequence events. While scenario analysis can take the form of robust statistical studies of different futures, experience suggests that preparation of qualitative narratives can oftentimes better capture contingencies and only partially foreseeable eventualities. Box 4.3 provides an illustrative example of a scenario analysis called the Great Transition developed by the Global Scenario Group.

Box 4.3: Global Scenario Group's Great Transition

In 2002, a group of sustainability scientists working under the umbrella of two policy think-tanks, the Stockholm Environment Institute and the Tellus Institute, published a widely disseminated report entitled *Great Transition: The Promise and Lure of the Times Ahead*. The authors conceptualize three worldviews that they term

Conventional Worlds, Barbarization, and *Great Transitions.* They subdivide each of these general perspectives into two scenarios for a total of six future-oriented archetypes.

First, Conventional Worlds, essentially a hopeful extension of the status quo, yields *Market Forces* based on continued reliance on self-correcting markets and *Policy Reform* which depends on government action to facilitate a sustainable future.

Second, the Barbarization worldview is decidedly pessimistic in outlook and anticipates a future characterized by two variants. One is termed *Breakdown,* which is a prospective state of continual conflict where crises spiral out of control and institutions collapse. A second option is *Fortress World,* a scenario that entails an authoritarian response in the face of risks posed by systemic organizational failures. In this alternative, we experience a world that takes on the qualities of global apartheid, where elites live in protected gated communities and everyone else is subjected to protracted poverty and violence.

Finally, the study offers the opportunity for a Great Transition comprising two variants. *Eco-communalism,* echoing the narrative advanced by visionaries like E. F. Schumacher, is a bioregional and localist idyll where people build strong democratic institutions and focus their attentions on proximate challenges. A second, arguably more realistic, alternative is termed the *New Sustainability Paradigm* which is centered on creating a just and humane global civilization predicated on international solidarity, cross-cultural understanding, and economic connectedness.

While by no means easily attainable, the New Sustainability Paradigm in many respects offers the most desirable future. The authors of *Great Transition* observe that to achieve this scenario two highly uncertain transformations will be required. We first must embark on a decades-long ecotechnological revolution of unprecedented magnitude and scale to reduce the burdens that contemporary activities impose on the biosphere. The developmental arc will then need to be bent a second time, and this undertaking will require deep reconsideration of human ambitions. The report concludes by observing that this is "the promise and the lure of the global future."

Source: Paul Raskin, Tariq Banuri, Gilberto Gallopín, Pablo Gutman, ... Rob Swart, 2002. *Great Transition: The Promise and Lure of the Times Ahead*. Boston, MA: Stockholm Environment Institute-Boston, 2002: https://www.tellus.org/tellus/publication/great-transition-the-promise-and-lure-of-the-time-ahead.

Second, robust processes of *future visioning* are a prerequisite for a more sustainable future. In other words, we must first create conceptions of more environmentally tenable and socially equitable worlds in our collective mind before we can begin to devise practical expressions of them. Developing common understanding entails visualization that can be carried out with varying levels of formalization. At one end of this continuum, political parties, for instance, typically offer visions of how they will govern if elected by their constituents. Because of the need to appeal to people of different persuasions and with often-divergent priorities, it is common for visions of this type to be communicated in relatively vague terms. At the other end, visions developed by certain organizations may be tantamount to a strategic plan with explicit targets and outputs. Given current purposes, the following discussion charts a middle path that describes a mode of visioning that is sufficiently tangible but does not become a straightjacket and affords opportunity for course correction over time.

Stakeholders who have a direct interest in the envisaged future generally are in the best position to partake in a visioning exercise. Importantly, at least initially, it is useful not to allow alleged obstacles or timeworn understandings to stand in the way, and participants should engage with a fertile imagination, all with the aim of reaching a loosely constructed consensus so that there is broad ownership of the outcome. The undertaking should be ambitious and not prematurely eliminate from consideration alternatives deemed to be impractical or unrealizable. The emphasis should be less on devising strategic and practicable pathways, as those considerations will typically come later in the process (see below). Throughout, it is important to stay focused on the "big picture" rather than to become overwhelmed by details. The appropriate scale can be a company, a neighborhood, a city, or other grouping that shares a common purpose, and the planning horizon is best set at approximately 25 years.

Future visioning should not be confused with forecasting or extrapolating current conditions out to a fixed date. It is important to encourage participants to focus on desirable futures that offer opportunities to realize ambitions and hence may depart from conceptions that are judged to be plausible or likely. Facilitators should not overly emphasize untoward or negative outcomes, as this pursuit will prompt participants to avoid engaging with the appropriate level of seriousness and commitment. People do not just want to avoid threats, but ultimately to strive to embrace futures that afford opportunities to flourish (see Box 4.4).

Box 4.4: Swedish energy system beyond 2020

In 2016, the Swedish Energy Agency published a report entitled *Four Futures: The Energy System Beyond 2020*. The document was the result of a visioning exercise that formulated four scenarios and assigned names to them based on musical performance types: *Forte*, *Legato*, *Espressivo*, and *Vivace*. A notable feature of the project is that its authors did not focus solely on the underlying technologies, but sought to connect specific modes of energy production with social organization, urban design, transportation, and lifestyles. The descriptions are based on both quantitative and qualitative analyses and include a combination of textual renderings, graphical presentations, and video vignettes depicting a "day-in-the-life" of representative people.

First, *Forte* (forceful) privileges low energy prices and the availability of ample supplies, especially for industry. Societal well-being is premised on economic growth and the widespread availability of employment in customary sectors.

Second, *Legato* (smooth, flowing) devotes priority to environmental sustainability and global justice. Accordingly, the government plays a major role in shifting energy production from centralized sources of supply to renewable sources.

Third, *Espressivo* (expressive) replaces fossil fuels and nuclear power with renewable energy, but the driving impulse is premised on individual initiative and responsiveness with an emphasis on ensuring flexibility and decentralization.

Finally, *Vivace* (lively) operationalizes the notion of green growth, which stresses reduction in greenhouse-gas emissions but in the context of ensuring continued reliance on customary lifestyles. This is achieved through development of extensive export markets for advanced environmental technologies and new bio-based industries.

While each of the scenarios results in important environmental improvements, only *Legato* and *Vivace* are deemed sufficient to enable Sweden to meet its climate targets and to facilitate a successful sustainability transition.

Source: Swedish Energy Agency, *Four Futures: The Energy System Beyond 2020*. Stockholm: Swedish Energy Agency, 2016: http://www.energimyndigheten.se/en/sustainability/four-futures.

Finally, *backcasting* is a normative planning method that is often deployed as a complement to scenario analysis, future visioning, and other futures studies methodologies. Sustainability scientist John Robinson (1982, 1988) described the concept in the 1980s, but he attributes the actual origins to work on soft energy paths carried out by Amory Lovins a decade earlier (see Chapter 3). As the name suggests, the technique is the opposite of forecasting in the sense that the latter starts from a current state and extrapolates forward in time. By contrast, backcasting entails formulation of an expectant outcome and then works in reverse to identify the intermediary steps that could constitute a pathway to connect prospective to current conditions. Robinson (1982) himself observes that "[t]he major difference is that backcasts are not intended to indicate what the future will likely be, but to indicate the relative implications of different policy goals." Applied in the context of energy alternatives, he contends that "[t]he purpose of backcasting is not to produce a planning blueprint but to indicate the relative feasibility and implications of different energy futures." Aside from assessing various options for energy policy, backcasting has been extensively used in urban planning and resource management (see, for example, Höjer et al. 2011).

In recent years, so-called participatory backcasting (or more formally termed participatory scenario-based backcasting) has achieved popularity among sustainability scientists as a technique that directly engages a range of stakeholders and fosters social learning. The aim is to create opportunities for diverse groups to contribute their voices to the exercise and to encourage expansive collective ownership of the consultation and eventual outcome. While participatory backcasting holds important advantages from the standpoint of democratic collaboration, the involvement of disparate communities raises methodological concerns, specifically to ensure that participants do not become beleaguered. It is furthermore important to build into the process adequate opportunity for people to acquire necessary technical expertise. Despite these obstacles, several notable studies involving participatory backcasting have been carried out in recent years as part of "climate futures" research projects. This work has focused on urban sustainability and the retrofitting central cities (Eames et al. 2013), land-use planning to achieve climate neutrality (Milestad et al. 2014), changes in consumer food practices (Davies 2014), and climate adaptations in coastal regions (Van der Voorn et al. 2012) (see Box 4.5).

Box 4.5: Retrofit 2050

Urban planner Malcolm Eames and colleagues carried out a project called Retrofit 2050 that involved participatory backcasting and foresight process scenarios to examine alternatives for retrofitting several city-regions in the United Kingdom. The backcasting portion of the project entailed three workshops conducted in 2011 and 2012 involving (1) problem framing and structuring, (2) visioning, and (3) pathway analysis. The facilitators recruited 32 experts from industry, academia, national and local government, government agencies, and civil society and community organizations whose role it was to assess the work carried out by the project team.

The backcasting and visioning process required envisaging how an existing city-region could be retrofit to become a sustainable urban environment. Through a process that involved conducting workshops with the expert advisory group, three broad "regimes" (comprising housing, non-domestic buildings, and urban infra-structure and land use) were conceptualized.

First, the *smart-networked city* is organized around a centralized hub and a highly mobile and globally competitive society. The city is fully integrated with advanced information and communication technologies and operates with a high level of efficiency due to the extensive use of intelligent control systems that optimize facilities operations. The city is outward looking and reliant on extensive mobility of people, goods, and services.

Second, the *compact city* is a dense configuration of land uses, buildings, and services and enables intensive and efficient urban lifestyles. Because of the degree of centralization, energy and resource use is significantly curtailed. The high density reduces developmental pressure on outlying areas that can be protected and preserved for their ecosystem services and recreational opportunities.

Finally, the *self-reliant green city* is an autonomous bioregion that maintains its ecological integrity and operates as a circular economy. Demand for energy and resources is low due to widespread public emphasis on materially sufficient lifestyles. Relatively speaking, this is an inward-looking society, but there is a global consciousness due to recognition of the need to respect planetary boundaries.

While these scenarios represent three "ideal types," they should not be regarded as singular and self-contained alternatives. It is more constructive to regard their defining features as prospective outcomes that are determined by explicit choices. Understood in such terms, the scenarios are "guiding visions" that can contribute to societal dialogues on how we can shape the future.

Source: Malcolm Eames, Tim Dixon, Tim May, and Miriam Hunt, City futures: Exploring urban retrofit and sustainable transitions, *Building Research and Information* 41(5) (2013): 504–516.

Cities and Sustainability Transitions

Cities have long served as centers for innovation, a historic pattern that is attributable to their role as nodes that aggregate diverse sources of knowledge, institutional resources, managerial expertise, and financial capital. Numerous analyses have identified urban centers as especially important geographic settings for sustainability transitions because they are points of convergence for multiple sociotechnical systems that organize contemporary modes of consumption and production (see, for example, De Haan et al. 2014; Rohracher and Späth 2014; Swilling and Hajer 2017). Especially relevant are transportation systems, energy systems, agro-food systems, public water systems, and stormwater-management systems, as well as regulatory and legal systems for overseeing land use, building, and construction. Often operated by municipal governments or public authorities, these sociotechnical systems simultaneously enable and circumscribe the provisioning practices of households, business firms, and others.[3] Moreover, because of both poor maintenance and inadequate investment in new facilities there are significant opportunities for enhancement of their sustainability performance. There is, furthermore, ample evidence to demonstrate that municipal governments, especially in several of the world's largest and most affluent cities, are already actively engaged in embracing the necessary challenges.

More than other places, cities are on the frontlines of sustainability. By 2050, more than 70 percent of the global population will be urban and because of higher incomes the residents of cities are generally responsible for consuming disproportionate volumes of energy and materials – and disgorging similarly oversized amounts of waste (including greenhouse-gas emissions embodied in consumer products). There is little question that cities will need to be the vanguard of the social and technological changes necessary to achieve a more sustainable future.

A considerable amount of attention has been devoted in recent years to the use of increased utility rates to reduce consumption of electricity and water, though the capacity of such policies to motivate system innovation has been quite limited. Furthermore, there is the risk that raising costs on basic services will have outsized impacts on lower-income households. An area where this general strategy has been used to positive effect has been through the imposition of so-called congestion pricing. This policy involves constructing an electronic cordon around the center of a city and requiring drivers to pay a fixed fee to enter the circumscribed zone (generally limited to specific hours of the day and days of the week). There is often a discount or exemption for electric vehicles or other special categories. At the time of this writing, the daily congestion charge in London and Stockholm is the equivalent of, respectively, $15.10 and $6.30.[4]

A similar policy measure involves increasing parking fees and/or reducing the amount of urban land devoted to the temporary storage of automobiles. The objective of such measures is to make it more expensive to warehouse cars on property that in many instances can be allocated to other purposes, thus increasing urban density and reducing the number of vehicles circulating on city streets. When municipal officials distribute the revenue generated by such demand-management schemes to new investments in public transportation, there is a stronger likelihood of triggering changes in travel behavior that can contribute to a sustainability transition. It must be acknowledged, though, that decisions to use financial tools to change user behavior, like any policy initiative, are filtered through a political process that can undermine ultimate effectiveness.

Urban planners are also implementing more ambitious concepts designed to break the lock-in of relatively low-density development patterns and to reduce automobile dependency. A particularly popular strategy entails the construction of so-called "transit-oriented developments" (sometimes termed "smart growth" or "transit villages") that co-locate public transportation with high-density residential and commercial facilities. Growing numbers of cities are also creating car-free zones and reallocating parts of roadways to the exclusive use of bicycle riders, pedestrians, and operators of other non-motorized modes of travel.[5] Substantial reduction in vehicular use has the potential to generate sustainability benefits by decreasing automobile-related fatalities and injuries, improving population health and well-being, and increasing community social connectivity.

Even more audacious have been plans to design "smart cities" that involve the installation of extensive networks of electronic sensors, cameras, and other digital technologies that capture information on the flow of materials and people as they move through urban environments (Kitchin 2014). The further aim is to develop the necessary computing capacity for analysis of the resultant data and to infuse the output into management systems to optimize usage of infrastructure and other municipal services.[6] While there is no single definition of a smart city, the general idea is that cities can harness the power of advanced information and communication technologies (ICTs) to become more efficient, and this improvement will lead to enhanced livability and economic competitiveness.

The instrumentation to enable a smart city can be ubiquitously built into the fabric of the city – sidewalks, traffic intersections, bridges, buildings, sewage pipes, and so forth – and via wireless transmission, which conveys information on activity levels and creates opportunities for continuous monitoring via mobile computing devices. The data can then be made available to both municipal managers and ordinary residents who can utilize it to make "smarter" real-time decisions about travel and other daily routines (see Box 4.6).

Perhaps unsurprisingly, the widespread enthusiasm surrounding smart cities has led to incisive critiques asserting that the underlying technologies are insidious and that, by focusing so strenuously on efficiency, the general concept actually undermines rather than enhances urban sustainability. Critics charge that the installation of pervasive sensing equipment across an entire city is an invasive form of public surveillance (sometimes termed the "panoptic society") and that collection of copious volumes of data on urban lifeways gives extraordinary power to the technology companies that are the most vigorous champions of the concept. Other skeptics of smart cities dismiss the undertaking as a form technological determinism that is similar to the various modes of ecological modernization discussed in Chapter 3.[7] Given this overwhelming emphasis, issues of social sustainability – equity and inclusion in particular – are given short shrift due to overwhelming emphasis on business-friendly priorities.

Despite the dominant way in which the smart city concept is currently being operationalized in many parts of the world, there is evidence emerging that ICTs can also be used to enable a more genuine and humane conception of sustainability anchored in the pursuit of improving individual and societal well-being. For example, Gregory Trencher and Andrew Karvonen (2019) invoke the notion of Smart City 2.0; they describe the cases of Kashiwanoha Smart City and Aizuwakamatsu Smart City in Japan, where residents use wearable health monitors and rely on open-data platforms to communicate virtually with medical practitioners. In another example, Francesca Cellina and colleagues (2020) describe how design of a new mobility app as part of a local living lab experiment in the Swiss city of Bellinzona prompted a tradition-bound municipal government to embrace a process

Box 4.6: Google's smart city in Toronto

Sidewalk Labs, a subsidiary of Google's parent company, Alphabet, had been seeking to build the ultimate smart city on a 12-acre lakefront site in Toronto, until the project was canceled in May 2020. The project, called Quayside, was to occupy a property that previously served as a shipping facility and was slated to consist of several 30-story mixed-use buildings, with 40 percent of the residential units designated as "affordable housing." The community was envisioned to be connected to the metro system by a light-rail line and to include a variety of public amenities, including heated pavements to keep the pedestrian and bicycling paths free of ice and snow during the winter. In keeping with its moniker to be "smart," Quayside was due to be outfitted with a variety of sensor systems to gauge energy consumption, waste disposal, traffic patterns, and other urban activities (including seating on individual park benches). A centralized management system would instantly analyze incoming data to provide residents with real-time feedback on fluctuations in activity.

Even before it was canceled, Quayside was mired in controversy. Particularly contentious were plans for handling the vast amounts of data generated by the development's daily operations. Sidewalk Labs had proposed the establishment of a third party "data trust" to provide transparency and to design protocols for how information would be shared. This arrangement, however, did not allay the concerns of privacy advocates, and the matter was being litigated. Further complications were created by what critics characterized as an undemocratic and secretive planning process that limited decision-making to a small cadre of Google managers and government officials.

Politically active Torontonians saw the disputes as an opportunity not only to shape Quayside, but to establish a template for how municipal governments around the world might work with ICT companies on the design and creation of smart cities. Also at issue was how the proceeds of intellectual property – including relevant artificial intelligence systems – would be distributed between residents and investors.

Source: Nancy Scola, Google is building a city of the future in Toronto: Would anyone want to live there? *Politico Magazine*, July/August 2018: https://www. politico.com/magazine/story/2018/06/29/google-city-technology-toronto-canada-218841.

of participatory planning that led to far-reaching consideration of future mobility scenarios.

Deep Transitions

A new development by researchers engaged in work on sociotechnical transitions entails the notion of "Deep Transitions," which brings together ideas from economic history, sociology, science and technology studies, and innovation studies. Formulated to date principally by historian Johan Schot and social theorist Laur Kanger, the perspective builds on several prior evolutionary conceptions and is focused on large-scale and long-term sociotechnical systems change. It aims to explain "how individual sociotechnical systems have historically become connected into complexes of systems, developed traction in particular directions, and how these complexes, in turn, have increasingly become part of the socio-material fabric of our economies, polities, cultural frameworks, social interactions and everyday practices" (Schot and Kanger 2018: 1046; see also Kanger and Schot 2019).

First, the notion of Deep Transitions draws on the idea of the "double movement" advanced during the 1940s by economic historian and social philosopher Karl Polanyi (2001 [1944]) as part his larger conception of a Great Transformation. Polanyi is still renowned today for outlining a dialectical process that initially begins with a "first movement" driven by industrialization and the expansion of laissez-faire economic policies that intensified social hardship. The "second movement" was then a reactionary response to these conditions and resulted in formation of the welfare state to reinstitute to varying degrees prior conditions of economic and environmental security.

Second, Schot and Kanger build on the foundations of economic historian Carlota Perez's concept of techno-economic paradigm (TEP) shifts, which is itself based on Schumpeterian-type long-wave dynamics (see, for example, Perez 2002). More specifically, the TEP framework asserts that periodically – and with a high level of regularity and hence predictability – clusters of interrelated innovations occur with respect to the technological, institutional, and organizational features of a society. These changes in turn drive increases in productivity and new modes of production and consumption as well as shifts in political alignment and cultural sensibilities. Each wave emerges slowly (and often locally) and over time builds in strength and geographic extent. The TEP framework constitutes five wave-like "great surges of development" since the onset of the Industrial Revolution, each one characterized by its own emblematic techno-economic paradigm.[8] Schot and Kanger (2018: 1047) refer to these paradigms as "meta-regimes," which they describe as "a coordinating mechanism generating interconnections between technologies and industries."

Because agents of financial capital have more flexibility than agents of production capital (which includes machines, factories, and so forth), the former are typically in the vanguard of shifting assets from a decaying paradigm to an emergent one. The promise of high returns leads to a "frenzy phase" with large amounts of capital being pumped into highly uncertain ventures, some of which are able to achieve success and spur the innovation of novel technologies. However, the general infusion leads to the creation – and eventual bursting – of a socially disruptive speculative bubble and eventual recession. To overcome this situation, there is pressure for regulatory intervention by government to stabilize the emergent sociotechnical system, which by this point has mostly displaced its predecessor. At this stage of solidifying maturity, the new configuration stabilizes and becomes a source of wealth expansion and decreasing income inequality. In due course, though, the availability of lucrative financial returns for capital dissipates and the cycle starts anew. Perez (2002) asserts – in ways that resemble the contentions of the Fourth Industrial Revolution proponents discussed in Chapter 3 – that we are in the incipient phase of a new surge in which ICTs begin to fuse with sustainability imperatives.[9]

Finally, the deep transition concept is constructed using key elements of the MLP as discussed above and Schot and Kanger contend that it helps to address several of the weaknesses and blind spots inherent in the TEP. For instance, the MLP includes a much wider array of actors than just financial and production capital and internalizes the conflicts that characterize the dynamic relationship between incumbent regimes and insurgent niches. In addition, the MLP – through the notion of the landscape – is more attentive to how external events and circumstances can enable transitions by opening windows of opportunity for the niche-based activities. The limitations of the MLP reside in the fact that it is largely centered on individual sociotechnical systems and its more myopic focus creates disconnections with larger macroeconomic and historical currents.

The notion of Deep Transitions begins by noting that the current double challenge is characterized by pronounced environmental degradation and perverse levels of social inequality and that fundamental change needs to be pursued from the standpoint of sociotechnical systems that span production, distribution, and consumption. Where this perspective departs from customary conceptions of sustainability transitions is that, rather than transformation of individual systems, the emphasis is on understanding processes of coordinated change across multiple systems. A Deep Transition is thus defined as "a series of connected and sustained fundamental transformations of a wide range of socio-technical systems in a similar direction" (Schot and Kanger 2018: 1045). More specifically, sociotechnical shifts are the result of synchronous and mutually interdependent improvements in labor productivity, fossil-fuel reliance, and development of global value chains. In other words, change does not emanate ultimately from idiosyncratic technological innovations and organizational advancements, but rather results from "connections between change processes in multiple systems [that take] on wave-type properties, unfolds through centuries, and is implicated in broader transformations of societies and economies" (Schot and Kanger 2018: 1045).

An important distinction between the idea of Deep Transitions and other theories based on sequential waves of innovation is that each groundswell does not constitute a new period of disruption and eventual reorganization. The claim instead is that within a particular centuries-long period, the successive surges actually constitute cumulating "layering" and "deepening" of emblematic techno-organizational characteristics. Schot and Kanger use the term "sedimentation" to describe this additive process and to suggest that the past 200–250 years have been marked not by multiple (and discontinuity creating) transitions, but rather by a single persistent process of industrialization and modernization that is tantamount to Polanyi's Great Transformation.[10] Understood in such terms, it is less the specific technologies in the narrow sense that impel a Deep Transition and more the "rule-systems" that establish the general direction of society as a whole and how rules and sociotechnical systems are seen as mutually constitutive. The simultaneously interlocking and consecutive configuration of sociotechnical systems (and their associated rules) that developed and diffused globally during the nineteenth and twentieth centuries is termed the First Deep Transition. While this process generated "unprecedented levels of wealth and welfare in the Western world," (Schot and Kanger 2018: 1046), it was also characterized by emblematic problems, including the creation of enormously wasteful systems of production and consumption, pollution, climate change, and widespread inequality (partially reversed during the middle decades of the twentieth century), and recurrent episodes of unemployment.

While there were, in hindsight, harbingers of an emergent need for new rules, awareness of the harmful outcomes propagated by the extant metasystem – or system of systems – did not start to become readily apparent until the 1960s and 1970s, when analyses like Rachel Carson's *Silent Spring* and the Club of Rome's *Limits to Growth* became influential. The diffusion of this understanding occurred along a disjointed and interrupted pathway, but Schot and Kanger (2018: 1046) contend that "these concerns have created increasing pressures on existing socio-technical systems, thereby stimulating possibilities for the emergence of the Second Deep Transition."

They further observe that this transformation entails "an overhaul of the directionality of the First Deep Transition and therefore the most fundamental principles guiding the mode of operation of socio-technical systems constituting modern societies" (2018: 1046). They are careful to qualify this contention by noting that, in accordance with the MLP, these changes are not systemic or mainstream but are rather occurring in particular niches as "an undercurrent of historical change" (2018: 1046). They point to advances in renewable energy, alternative food movements, and novel mobility services as evidence of this process. However, the acceleration of these nascent developments will require active engagement by governments in the form of robust facilitating policies and intermediation by a range of actors, including NGOs, civil society organizations, multinational corporations, and others. At the same time, eventual stabilization is not predetermined but will be conditioned by a variety of events including speculative bubbles and other systemic shocks such as war, political upheavals, and climate change. The larger point is that contemporary sustainability challenges cannot be resolved by the current rule-system but, rather, will require a series of reinforcing surges that enable a fundamental shift that "undermine[s] the very principles of production, distribution, and consumption on which the First Deep Transition is based" (2018: 1057).

How might we recognize the emergence of the precursors of a Second Deep Transition that allows for a breakthrough out of industrial modernity? Schot and Kanger (2018) suggest that indications could include a historical shift from mass manufacturing for global markets to socially useful and craft-based production for local communities, from linear economies reliant on fossil fuels to zero-waste provisioning organized around circular systems of materials management, and from individual to collective consumption. We can also add to this list a transformation in dominant understanding of prosperity that singularly stresses wealth accumulation to an emphasis on fulfillment and flourishing as well as replacement of preoccupations favoring efficiency with newfound commitments premised on sufficiency. Put more succinctly, it will likely be necessary to develop a new understanding of progress.

Conclusion

The various perspectives on sociotechnical transitions described in this chapter are in many respects extensions and elaborations of the theory of ecological modernization discussed in Chapter 3. While acknowledging that efforts outlined above to impel system innovation are more attentive to complexity and contingency and embrace a wider range of societal influences, both approaches are notable for their commitment to managerial steering, technological inventiveness, effective governance, and adaptive planning. Whether focused on reforming extant provisioning systems for energy, housing, mobility, food, or water, the implicit conviction is that "We can do this!"

These modernist conceptions have coalesced for the most part in Northern Europe and they have been heavily influenced by the cultural and institutional characteristics of this particular region. The constituent countries subscribe to what is often termed the "European social model" and demonstrate comparatively strong commitment to state-sponsored policy planning, corporatist decision-making, and social protection. The point is not to imply homogeneity across these nations, because important differences do indeed exist, but rather to contend that interest in and capacity for sociotechnical transitions derive from a specific array of historical circumstances. In short, the United States is not Sweden and the United Kingdom is not Denmark, and we should not presume that conceptual frameworks developed primarily in one context can be straightforwardly applied elsewhere.

Despite the important insights that an emphasis on sociotechnical innovation provides, several critical issues are largely excluded from its purview. For instance, researchers and policy practitioners tend to avoid focusing on the need to realign incentives in the finance industry with sustainability, to scale back current emphasis on pervasive product promotionalism and unremittingly consumerist lifestyles, and to reconsider capitalism as an efficacious system of societal organization. In other words, it is insufficient to engage in efforts to supplant prevailing provisioning arrangements without also accounting for the still more expansive sets of rules and norms in which they are embedded. The customary response to this critique is that such issues are part of the landscape as understood by the MLP. However, this macro-level tier tends to receive insufficient attention in terms of how its evolutionary trajectory could be redirected – perhaps through more assertive and strategic engagement of intergovernmental institutions – to enable a more environmentally tenable and socially equitable future.

Another reason for skepticism about the extent to which we can deliberately steer sociotechnical transitions centers on the tendency of most analyses of system innovation to underplay the political dimensions. Implicit in efforts to activate transformational processes is the conceit that there is broad societal consensus on the need to enhance the environmental and social performance of contemporary systems of consumption and production. Especially during a period when the rise of authoritarianism poses pronounced threats to democratic governance and political legitimacy remains inexorably tethered to customary measures of economic growth, it is imperative to inquire whether sustainability is actually a globally salient objective. Accordingly, it merits recognizing that resistance is not necessarily motivated by lack of understanding or cynicism but rather by correct appraisal of how anticipated changes will adversely affect the well-being of particular people and communities. We thus may be looking at a situation in which the countries of Northern Europe manage to achieve a regionally circumscribed sustainability transition while the rest of the world muddles along in much the same way that it has for the past several decades.[11]

In other words, the prospect of sociotechnical transitions taking hold across a broad expanse of society can provide a compelling and generally optimistic vision, but the envisaged system innovations are likely to unfold on a patchy and irregular basis. In the absence of invigorated political commitments demanding sharp curtailment of greenhouse-gas emissions and aggressive efforts to address other global-scale sustainability challenges, these transformational processes will not overtly touch most people. They will instead continue to be buffeted by climate change and other perils with perhaps a small margin of economic and environmental security provided by indiscriminately implemented technological improvements.

5

Social Innovation and Sustainability

Introduction

The concept of a social problem was first formalized early in the twentieth century by the American sociologist Hornell Hart. In an article entitled "What is a social problem?" he set forth the following definition:

> A social problem is a problem which actually or potentially affects large numbers of people in a common way so that it may best be solved by some measure or measures applied to the problem as a whole rather than by dealing with each individual as an isolated case, or which requires concerted or organized human action. (1923: 349)

This formulation led to the establishment of a specialization within the discipline of sociology specifically devoted to the study of social problems. Hart divided the field into four categories: economic problems (how to narrow the gap between poverty and excessive wealth), health problems (how to extend the life span and provide universal access to healthcare), political and sociopsychological problems (how to make human relationships more conducive to societal well-being), and educational problems (how to enable people to have enriched lives and contribute to society). He was certain that through the careful efforts of appropriately trained experts, the development of integrated science, and the establishment of sufficiently comprehensive databases, it would be possible to make steady progress in addressing the most seemingly intractable social problems.

A provocative and widely heralded treatment of the concept exactly a half-century later by the city planners Horst Rittel and Melvin Webber (1973: 155) advanced a very different view of how to handle social problems:

> The search for scientific bases for confronting problems of social policy is bound to fail, because of the nature of these problems. They are "wicked" problems, whereas science has developed to deal with "tame" problems. Policy problems cannot be definitely described. Moreover, in a pluralistic society there is nothing like the undisputable public good, there is no objective definition of equity, policies that respond to social problems cannot be meaningfully correct or false, and it makes no sense to talk about "optimal solutions" to social problems unless severe qualifications are imposed first. Even worse, there are no "solutions" in the sense of definitive and objective answers.

Especially among the growing ranks of critical social scientists, Rittel and Webber's brand of subjectivism – some might even call it nihilism – was greeted with a mostly positive response. It also resonated with grassroots social activists, alternative technology proponents, and both progressive and libertarian political movements. Unsurprisingly, it did not find much sympathy within mainstream institutions or, indeed, among the public as a whole. Despite harboring certain doubts about the value of expertise, most people at the time retained a strong commitment to customary understandings of progress and continual improvement (Crowley and Head 2017).

Notwithstanding certain setbacks caused by a range of failures both large and small, as well as the emergence of modestly sized pockets of dissent, the following decades gave rise to developments that reaffirmed the role of experts – particularly technological specialists – in addressing, and perhaps even resolving, social problems.[1] An especially audacious example of this tendency was an article published in *Forbes* magazine a few years ago under the headline "Solving Social Problems: 11 Ways New Tech Can Help" (Forbes Technology Council 2017).[2] The commentary then proceeded to identify how digital tools could be especially effective in addressing dilemmas related to, for instance, healthcare, access to clean drinking water, and agriculture, as well as perhaps less obvious issues such as loneliness among seniors, voter participation, and poverty.

Business leaders are not the only societal members who maintain allegiance to this commitment. For instance, the OECD has long been active in recasting social problems as technical problems and convening conferences and publishing reports to reinforce this allegiance (see, for example, OECD 2011). There are, of course, powerful reasons for inter-governmental bodies to champion such ideas. This posture can effectively shift responsibility for difficult issues away from the political sphere, redefine liabilities as opportunities, and create potentially lucrative openings for companies in search of new markets. There are surely differences in the relative emphasis that countries place on these objectives, though some analysts have suggested that the United States has a unique penchant for embracing technological solution-seeking (Nye et al. 2014; Segal 2017).[3]

This situation has become emblematic of current efforts to address sustainability challenges. Social problems that are ultimately attributable to poorly designed economic incentives, overly individualized consumption practices, ineptly conceived land-use regulations, and so forth are deemed too difficult to resolve through processes of democratic governance. Policymakers then hand off the resultant problems to applied scientists and engineers to address as best they can through technological means. The most prominent contemporary example is climate change. This dilemma is, fundamentally speaking, a social problem caused by societal overreliance on fossil fuels and outsized production of green-house gases. However, the task of reducing contemporary reliance on carbon-intensive sources is widely considered excessively ambitious or frustrated by powerful political and economic interests with too much money invested in existing alternatives. Policymakers tend to regard social innovation premised on demand reduction as impractical and perverse, so the preferred approach has centered on seeking techno-logical breakthroughs. The leading approaches, as discussed in Chapter 3, have been to lower the carbon content of fossil fuels, to develop capacity for carbon capture and storage, to promote electric automo-bility, and to enhance the viability of geo-engineering.

Consistent with such an understanding, this book has devoted consid-erable attention to the potential of novel technologies to contribute to the pursuit of a more sustainable future. This chapter considers sustainability – or rather unsustainability – as a social problem. It shifts attention to the role of social innovation and the efforts of self-motivated individuals, grassroots organizations, and community groups to reduce resource utilization and encourage social equity. Many of these under-takings have necessarily been experimental and small in scale and have oftentimes encountered many of the obstacles that are common to startup enterprises of all kinds. At the same time, the scope and diversity of these ventures can be overwhelming. To keep this chapter to a manageable length, the discussion focuses on five partially overlapping propositions: sharing and collaborative consumption, self and communal provi-sioning, economic localization, minimalist lifestyles, and livelihoods in the era of digital automation. Importantly, readers should not construe the social innovations highlighted here as a comprehensive inventory and are encouraged to seek out activities taking place in their own neighborhood, as many communities have groups of spirited people involved in likeminded efforts. The conclusion gathers together key insights from these inspired initiatives.

Collaborative Consumption and the Sharing Economy

Home economists, feminists, and others have long recognized that the pooling of household and other consumer goods can enhance individual and societal well-being. The sharing of cars, household appliances, and clothing, as well as familial responsibilities like childcare and meal preparation, attenuates compulsion for ownership, reduces energy consumption, and enhances social solidarity. Even in relatively affluent countries, common usage was an unremarkable social practice throughout the first half of the twentieth century and in some communities proved laudably durable. However, once-routine forms of collaborative consumption began to dissipate in the decades following World War II as a result of rising affluence, expanding suburbanization, increasing individualization, growing emphasis on consumerist lifestyles, and falling relative prices for domestic equipment.[4]

Fast-forward to the early 2000s and the rapid proliferation of novel Internet capabilities, powerful and multifunctional smartphones, online payment for goods and services via credit card, mass use of global positioning systems, and online feedback to rate performance. For technology-savvy entrepreneurs, it was as if a new resource-rich territory affording lucrative commercial opportunities had just been opened up for settlement. The Great Recession that begin in 2007, and the millions of people who practically overnight found themselves without jobs, also prompted the launching of new business ventures as the recently unemployed became the casual labor that enabled nascent enterprises like Uber, Lyft, Airbnb, and many others to get off the ground.

Quick-moving venture capitalists sought to identify an area of social life where there was slack capacity – a partially utilized car, an empty bedroom, or a rarely worn dress – and to then encourage the creation of digital marketplaces where the forlorn item could be effortlessly matched to an eager user. When executed successfully, the arrangement produced a quadruple win: rental income from an underutilized product for the owner, convenient and affordable product access for the renter, commissions for the platform broker, and escalating valuations for the investor. Cultural scene-setters, academic pundits, and media commentators – and then proponents themselves – quickly started to herald these exchanges as the "sharing economy" (Botsman and Rogers 2010; Gansky 2010). This sunny appellation cast an extremely agreeable light on the incipient phenomenon, at least for a while, and supercharged the diffusion of business models premised on this idea.

Concomitantly, some sustainability specialists proclaimed the sharing economy to be an efficacious way to put productive assets to better use and to improve the efficiency of consumption. Other analysts asserted that the rise of these digital platforms – for better or worse – was a harbinger of revolutionary social change that presaged the end of consumer capitalism. This is clearly *not* how the shift to collaborative consumption has thus far unfolded. The main thrust of the "sharing economy" is better regarded as the "gig economy" and from the vantage point of sustainability is decidedly suspect. Just to take transportation as an example, ride-sharing has actually increased the number of cars on city streets, contributed to "hypermobile" travel practices, and exacerbated social inequality. The large gap between promise and achievement stems from the fact that most sponsors are single-mindedly fixated on using the online marketplaces to enhance accessibility and cost-effectiveness and, in many respects, they perform very well on this score.

Fortunately, this mostly disheartening situation is being partially offset by developments in more felicitous corners of the sharing/gig economy. We need to look past its most visible expressions (sometimes referred to as "Big Sharing") and the commitment of these firms to a logic dictated by venture capital investment and satisfaction of just-in-time consumer demand. Less obvious and celebrated are compelling examples of how efforts to foster mutualism and cooperation are enabling sustainable lifestyles. We can distinguish two different modes.

The first is *civic sharing*, which is a form of nonpecuniary provisioning that is much more prevalent than we might initially expect it to be. It includes public trains and buses as well as taxpayer-financed schools, libraries, and swimming pools. We do not always think about these facilities and services in terms of collective consumption, but they often fulfill critical communal needs and unquestionably add important value to our lives. Moreover, they play an essential role – and could play a larger one – addressing social problems such as lowering carbon footprints and reducing economic precarity. In other words, when we sever ownership from usership, it becomes possible to allocate responsibilities in ways that reduce material throughput, improve efficiency, and, if the system is artfully designed, encourage social solidarity and community engagement

Second, and still more germane from the standpoint of sustainability, is *communitarian sharing*, which is another nonpecuniary form of collaborative consumption based on genuine forms of mutuality. This category includes a broad assortment of activities that we can organize into four categories: housing, food, clothing, and cities.

First, the notion of "home" has been undergoing a process of dynamic restructuring in recent decades, as a result of, among other factors, demographic aging, declining fertility, economic and generational shifts, and evolving social norms. In addition, new conceptions of the family, financial constraints, and outmoded housing stocks are contributing to an increasingly problematic mismatch between residential needs and available options. The customary market-informed expectation is that housing providers would discern these changing requirements and adjust construction in accordance with evolving demand conditions. However, in most countries, conservative managerial mindsets, restrictive land-use controls, and community opposition have combined to limit the pace of these responses. In the face of such challenges, residents and housing advocates have organized their own forms of social innovation. Increasingly prevalent strategies are based on communitarian principles and include an array of shared-use living arrangements involving co-housing, community-based housing, and self-help and self-build housing. These initiatives are often led by civil society organizations working at a grassroots level, and in some countries – notably the United Kingdom and developing countries like Sri Lanka and Peru – have had commendable success owing to supportive policy frameworks that have provided funding and technical support.

Second, access to food is a fundamental and inseparable element of sustainability. Its cultivation, distribution, and preparation are responsible for more than one-third of global greenhouse-gas emissions, while, concurrently, these activities generate glaring inequalities and deficits in "food democracy" (Hassanein 2003; Vermeulen et al. 2012). SDG 2 is committed to "zero hunger" and asserts that "[a] profound change of the global food and agriculture system is needed if we are to nourish the 821 million people who are hungry today and the additional 2 billion people expected to be undernourished by 2050" (see Sachs 2012; Haddad 2015).

A diverse array of organizations around the world is getting involved in efforts to enhance food security through new and rediscovered communitarian projects: community gardens, gleaning, yard-farming, urban foraging, communal kitchens, and surplus food distribution. The characteristics of these sharing arrangements are extremely varied: some have established infrastructures, while others are more casual and fluid. It is, furthermore, important to acknowledge that some of these provisioning modes can raise statutory and regulatory issues pertaining to safety and hygiene, and there are regular conflicts with customary retailers who claim that these schemes constitute a source of unfair competition. Nonetheless, food-sharing offers interesting opportunities to reduce hunger and catalyze developments that can enhance equitable access to food (see Box 5.1; see also Box 4.2).

Box 5.1: Food swaps

Food swaps are communal events whereby participants meet in a private home or community center on a semiregular basis to exchange homegrown, homemade, and locally foraged foods. The format prohibits the use of cash; instead, swappers partake in a silent auction at which they initially declare interest in certain items that are on display before subsequently consummating the trades. For instance, two participants might agree to swap a jar of marmalade for a loaf of freshly baked bread. The events are a way for food-makers to diversify their pantries, exchange recipes, and distribute seasonal surpluses, while at the same time joining in an enjoyable social activity.

While the sharing of food is an age-old practice, lore holds that the first contemporary food swap was held in Brooklyn in 2010. The event took place during the shadow of the global financial crisis that struck two years earlier and the focus on locally produced artisanal food proved immensely popular. Word spread quickly and before long, food-swapping had become a mini social movement. Today, there are dozens of local swapping groups in the United States and elsewhere around the world.

Food swaps are a genuinely sustainable activity. They typically rely on locally procured ingredients and provide a forum for neighbors to get together to exchange knowledge. The events do not require the consumption of large amounts of energy and offer a convivial experience that builds community solidarity.

Source: Food Swap Network: https://foodswapnetwork.com.

Third, prior to the advent of ready-to-wear apparel, secondhand provisioning of clothes was a popular practice given the high cost of new attire. After an extended hiatus during the second half of the twentieth century, the acquisition of used clothing is again becoming increasingly common. Some municipal governments are even encouraging the establishment of specialized urban districts that serve as hubs for the buying, selling, and trading of previously owned garments, and designers are developing reuse systems based on circular-economy models. Under certain circumstances, extending the lifespan of textiles confers important benefits from the standpoint of sustainable materials management (Sandin and Peters 2018).

A facet of this trend that resonates with communitarian sharing and builds on food swaps is the organization of similar events involving clothing. Part rummage sale and part neighborhood party, such events are held at a host's home or other local venue and participants are encouraged to bring an assortment of used clothing to trade. The specific guidelines vary depending on logistics and size of the group, but the general idea is that there is an affable interchange of unwanted garments. Participants arrive with armloads of disused clothing and leave with an equitable number of treasured new finds. Organizers often convene the swaps as social gatherings or festivals, so there is a palpable emphasis on hospitality. As is the case for other modes of product reuse, the aim of these events is to keep goods circulating and to lessen consumer demand for replacement purchases, thus reducing landfill disposal and pressure on the need to manufacture anew.

Finally, several urban centers around the world, notably Seoul, Amsterdam, and Bangalore, have begun to take steps to envisage what it means to be a "sharing city." The aim is to redirect the commercial platforms toward public purpose and develop autonomous capabilities that municipal managers can then embed on a less proprietary basis into the fabric of communities in ways that enhance fairness and justice. Accordingly, the idea of a sharing city serves as a strategy to leverage interest in "smart cities" with other innovative concepts like social urbanism, urban communing, and just sustainability and to create an integrated planning framework (Agyeman and Evans 2004). Notable efforts to date include establishment of the Sharing Cities Alliance, the Sharing Cities Program (which operates in consultation with the European Innovation Partnership on Smart Cities and Communities), and the Sharing Cities Network hosted by Shareable (a website and social networking activator).[5]

Maker Movement and Self-Provisioning

The last several years have seen an explosion of interest in the so-called Maker Movement. Though the concept has deep historical roots, in its current usage it refers to an incredibly broad array of activities ranging from the making of beer, furniture, and designer crafts to the manufacture of industrial prototypes in commercial makerspaces, shared machine shops, and fabrication laboratories ("fab labs") (Gershenfeld

2005; Anderson 2012). The impulse behind this burst of ingenuity is attributable to the advent of new lifestyles that celebrate the acquisition and practice of creative skills and the availability of novel technologies like 3D printers and computer-operated laser-cutters. Policymakers have also identified self-provisioning as an opportunity to stimulate interest in STEM (science, technology, engineering, and math) fields, to revitalize vacant manufacturing districts, and to provide jobs for dislocated industrial workers. One recent survey estimates that there are currently 135 million makers in the United States alone, and the trend is further evinced by the extraordinary popularity of websites like Etsy that provide commercial venues for the sale of individually crafted goods.

Representatives of the World Economic Forum, prominent international consulting firms, and numerous others have heralded the Maker Movement as the incipient stage of a process that, in due course, will radically reconfigure familiar modes of production and consumption by shifting from centralized to distributed manufacturing. Closely associated with this envisaged transition are various related developments based on the notion of "prosumption," which points to a melding of the customary binary distinction between producers and consumers. The vision extends beyond the self-provisioning of ordinary household products, and anticipates that additive manufacturing and related technologies will soon allow for local fabrication of cars and even houses (see Box 5.2).

In the eyes of some of its proponents, the Maker Movement has significant potential from a sustainability standpoint, in part, because of what psychologists refer to as the "self-creation effect." The claim is that when consumers are alienated from the production of goods, they are inclined to be indifferent to their consequences. However, as makers become more engaged in the manufacture, as well as the eventual use, of products, they are disposed to be more attentive to the resultant social and environmental implications. Commenting on their study of this phenomenon, marketing analysts Johanna Brunneder and Utpal Dhalokia (2018: 387) observe that the self-creation effect "provides a concrete and compelling set of reasons why consumers should consider making products themselves instead of simply going to a store and purchasing ready-made items. It allows them to become active creators, to consume products prudently and consciously, to enjoy the consumption experience and to add to their well-being."

If the scaling up and proliferation of the Maker Movement were to be realized, it would unquestionably be an achievement of historic significance. However, it is important to take a step back and view its sustainability claims, at least, with a measure of skepticism. In the first instance, it is likely impractical to expect that the logistics of global supply

Box 5.2: Local Motors

Established in 2007, Arizona-based Local Motors is transforming the process for manufacturing cars. The company's business model relies on establishing "microfactories" that serve as facilities for the full range of operations – design, parts fabrication, vehicle assembly, and marketing. The combined factory-offices are approximately 50,000 square feet in size, about the same dimensions as a suburban supermarket. Local Motors is a leader in the use of 3D printing to manufacture electric cars in low volumes, and relies on a crowdsourced community to co-design and co-create new models. Because production plants are local, the company is able to tailor its vehicles to meet geographically specific requirements such as larger air conditioners in warm weather places and better traction in snowy locales.

The aim is to enable customers to select several customized components, including the exterior style, the type of powertrain, and various other options. The vehicle would then be produced locally and be ready to drive away the next day. In addition, the car is designed to be readily modifiable to accommodate the owner's evolving needs or to upgrade the vehicle by installing new technological improvements like a battery with more storage capacity.

Local Motors's most acclaimed current project centers on an autonomous minibus called Olli, which it manufactures using a large 3D printer and which integrates artificial intelligence from IBM's *Watson*, so that vehicles have the ability to speak directly to passengers. It is able to answer questions about its operations, navigational procedures, and safety maneuvers. The minibus can be produced in just 10 hours. It can accommodate a dozen passengers and travels at 15–18 miles per hour, which makes it suitable as a shuttle for city centers, college campuses, and other relatively modest-length routes.

Source: Local Motors: https://localmotors.com. Sean O'Kane, Local Motors wants to prove 3D-printed self-driving shuttles are safe, *The Verge*, March 8, 2019: https://www.theverge.com/2019/3/8/18255176/local-motors-olli-3d-printed-self-driving-shuttle-crash-test-footage.

chains and the economics of production will justify the self-manufacture of more than a trivial number of high value and customizable goods. Accordingly, most products will continue to be fabricated in low-cost locations and shipped to points of eventual use and consumption. As innovation scholar Jeremy Millard and his colleagues (2018) explain:

> [I]t will still be too expensive and cumbersome to meet the demands for very cheap standardized products and, in the context of growing world trade, standardization is critical to keep prices low as well as keep quality and reliability up. Thus, more likely is that manufacturing develops in two phases: the base products will be mass-manufactured, while finalization and personalization will happen in or close to the market, both geographically and culturally.

Moreover, actual evidence regarding the sustainability improvements of this purported new industrial revolution is, at least to date, decidedly mixed. Leading voices in the Maker Movement have evinced little tangible concern for reducing consumptive throughput or addressing the social and environmental ramifications of these activities to any significant degree. In addition, indications are that localized modes of prosumption are not expected to replace mass manufacturing but, rather, are likely to supplement it, thus leading to more rather than less utilization of energy and materials. Again, the observations of Millard et al. (2018) are powerful and persuasive. They observe that "there remains a significant gap between 'making,' on the one hand, and social and sustainable innovation on the other. Making is often still dominated by the latest gadgets, technical prowess, and playful experimentation which are of strategic importance for innovation."

This characterization raises the question of whether the Maker Movement, at least in its current manifestation, can be regarded as an effective sustainability strategy. An optimistic response is that a favorable outcome is possible, but proponents will need to develop an understanding of social transformation that goes beyond gee-whizz wonderment and unrestrained ardor for "the next big thing." Doing so also entails curtailing the commercialized facets of the Maker Movement that are expressly devoted to commodifying interest in self-manufacturing and maximizing financial returns for investors.

A Maker Movement that embraces and contributes meaningfully to sustainability could be enabled by giving credence to its dissident factions that owe their origins to the insights of pioneering thinkers like John Ruskin, William Morris, Buckminster Fuller, and Robert Pirsig. These visionaries are notable for advancing the view that the manual arts are not just an instrumental activity but, rather, provide an effective way to build resourcefulness and interest in purposeful living. The following discussion highlights three ways in which this alternative tradition is receiving contemporary expression.

First, some makers are reconciling the requirements of sustainability by fostering the transfer of do-it-yourself (DIY) skills through collaborative learning. A notable example in New York City is the Brooklyn Brainery, which describes itself as providing "accessible, community-driven, crowd-sourced education." The facility delivers short courses on an extensive array of topics, some practical and others more esoteric. A recent review of offerings included classes on glass etching, medieval art, knitting, and vegan cooking. Instructors do not necessarily need formal credentials, but instead possess a body of appropriate knowledge and a passion to share it with likeminded learners. The format is unpretentious and courses are meant to be fun and enjoyable, with small enrollments (about a dozen students) and short durations (one to four sessions).

Second, some observers allege that, in many respects, the Maker Movement approaches the challenge of sustainability from the wrong direction. The current dilemma is less a matter of where and how we manufacture consumer goods and more an issue of their durability and longevity. Product policies have long been predicated on the notion of premature obsolescence, which encourages designers to shorten lifespans and ensures overly rapid abandonment by consumers. A further problem is that the technological underpinnings of consumption have become a dark mystery for most ordinary people as they have lost the capacity to repair their own consumer goods. It was not always this way. When everyday items consisted of mechanical sub-assemblies, tinkerers with relatively modest proficiency could often complete routine fixes with a few common tools and a little ingenuity. A direct outcome of the electronics revolution – where even simple appliances now have embedded computerization – is that these undertakings have become much more difficult and oftentimes impossible. In many cases, we do not need maker-conceived innovations but, instead, more reliable ways to ensure the ongoing functionality of what we currently have on hand.

Most readers have probably at one time or another become frustrated when a recent purchase begins to fail after only a few weeks or months of use because, say, the battery does not properly recharge. A quick scan of the plastic casing leads one to find wording imploring the user not to tamper with the product because doing so will void any warranty or quality assurance. Further inspection is likely to reveal that there is, in any event, no obvious way to access the working parts of the device because the joints were soldered together at the factory. The ubiquity of this exasperating situation has given rise to nascent social mobilization around the related notions of "freedom to tinker" and "right to repair." As legal scholar Pamela Samuelson (2016: 564) observes:

People tinker with technologies and other human-made artifacts for a variety of reasons: to have fun, to be playful, to learn how things work, to discern flaws or vulnerabilities, to build their skills, to become more actualized, to tailor the artifacts to serve one's specific needs or functions, to repair or make improvements to the artifacts, to adapt them to new purposes, and, occasionally, to be destructive.

One aim of the tinkering/right-to-repair movement is to raise public awareness of ongoing efforts on the part of governments and consumer product companies to narrow the ability of users to interact with their possessions in the ways outlined above. Advocates have also been seeking to advance legislation that would establish a legal right to tinker.

Finally, a related development regarding the maintenance of consumer goods entails the establishment of so-called repair cafés, which are permanent or "pop-up" services where experts will fix everyday goods for a relatively modest fee. They operate either on a stand-alone basis or as part of occasional community events, and can be focused on electronics, clothing, or other product categories. Depending on the sort of service on offer, users drop off their defective appliances or torn garments, which are then returned in serviceable shape a few hours or days later. Some repair cafés even encourage users to participate directly as a way of sharing instruction and of opening up opportunities for community engagement.

An innovative online version of a repair café is iFixit, a California-based company that bills itself as the "Wikipedia of repair."[6] Established in 2003, when founder Kyle Wiens was unable to find a repair manual for his Apple iBook, iFixit provides instructional guides on how to fix thousands of consumer goods. Information is assembled by staff and volunteers and made available via the iFixit website in text and video formats. The company generates income by selling specialized tools and performing product teardowns (systematic disassembly to identify constituent components). In addition to empowering users to repair their own devices, the objective of iFixit is to reduce the volume of electronic waste relegated to landfills or exported to developing countries.

Economic Localization

Among many sustainability proponents, localization (or relocalization) has long ranked as one of the most important strategies for reducing throughput of energy and materials and fostering less resource-intensive lifestyles. While it had numerous antecedents, it was E. F. Schumacher's book, *Small Is Beautiful*, that married localism to environmentalism and triggered numerous social experiments in community-based lifestyles.

More recently, the concept has become widely deployed as a strategy for retail promotion and product labeling, to the extent that the notion of "local" has become in the minds of many people essentially tantamount to "sustainable." In fact, the practice is frequently – but not always correctly – conflated with other objectives that are variously connected to sustainability, including chemical-free, carbon-neutral, organic, safer, traceable, hand-produced, family-owned, ethical, and healthier (Feldman and Hamm 2015). The term is applied to an extensive array of products, ranging from tomatoes and wine to lumber used for homebuilding. It may also be the case that consumers prefer local alternatives because proximity conveys greater tangibility and empathy than other nominal signifiers of sustainability. This has especially been the case for food, which, despite various obstacles regarding seasonality and availability, has achieved significant prominence due to the proliferation of farmers' markets and other venues devoted to the distribution of locally produced vegetables, meat, and other foodstuffs.

Localization is a concept that has the power to turn ambivalent observers, or even erstwhile opponents, of sustainability into enthusiastic champions. For instance, municipal governments, chambers of commerce, civic organizations, farming advocates, and others who were initially reticent about endorsing the idea have become strongly supportive after realizing the commercial benefits that appeals to local provenance can generate.

While food occupies an especially prominent position in discussions of how to enhance the sustainability of contemporary provisioning practices, numerous other strategies are being pursued (see Box 5.3). Grassroots organizations around the world are involved in establishing, for example, community currency schemes, time banks, and barter networks (see the section above on collaborative consumption and the sharing economy). The objective of many of these initiatives is to increase what urban and regional economists refer to as the "multiplier effect" (the number of times that a unit of currency – say a dollar – is re-spent in a community) and, in a related vein, to reduce the amount of "leakage" (the outflow of money from the local economy). The general objective is to create more robust and interdependent social and economic linkages within a region that reduce the need for long-distance transactions between anonymous sellers and buyers. Writer and farmer Wendell Berry (1993: 17) captures the essence of localism:

> The real improvements then must come, to a considerable extent, from the local communities themselves. We need local revision of our methods of land use and production. We need to study and work together to reduce scale, reduce overhead, reduce industrial

Box 5.3: Local exchange trading systems

Local exchange trading systems (LETS) are schemes for enabling community-based forms of economic exchange that do not require the use of conventional currency. A local organization can print its own paper money in various denominations (more recently, it has taken the form of an electronic ledger) and participants then use this to facilitate transactions for goods and services. For instance, Joe could use the local currency to pay Lucy the equivalent of $20 for a haircut; Lucy, in turn, could spend this money on groceries at the community cooperative market. The managers of the market might subsequently pay a portion of the weekly salary of some of its worker-owners using the complementary currency.

A key advantage of LETS is that the value that accrues from interpersonal transactions is retained in the immediate geographic vicinity rather than being appropriated by nonlocal vendors and investors who have little enduring interest in the economic health of the community. In addition, participation in a LETS supports local businesses, while building familiarity with neighbors and enhancing social solidarity.

Precursors of contemporary LETS were introduced by social reformers during the early nineteenth century and the idea was popularized in the United States and elsewhere during the 1930s at the height of the Great Depression. Early proponents recognized that the demise of formal economic exchange at the time was not because of a lack of resourcefulness, but, rather, was attributable to the fact that people lacked legally issued currency. Hundreds of communities began printing their own local "script" and distributing it to residents as a way to enable local forms of exchange between, for instance, farmers and consumers.

An example of a successful LETS is Ithaca Hours, which has been operating in the modestly sized city of Ithaca, New York, since 1991; in recent years, the scheme has entered into an alliance with the local Alternatives Credit Union. Participants contend that they are "making a community while making a living" and striving to "relieve the social desperation which has led to compulsive shopping and wasted resources." Ithaca Hours and other LETS are aligned with the Schumacher Center for New Economics.

Source: Ithaca Hours: http://www.ithacahours.com. Schumacher Center for a New Economics: https://centerforneweconomics.org.

dependencies; we need to market and process local products locally; we need to bring local economies into harmony with local ecosystems so that we can live and work with pleasure in the same places indefinitely; we need to substitute ourselves, our neighborhoods, our local resources, for expensive imported goods and services; we need to increase cooperation among all local economic entities: households, farms, factories, banks, consumers, and suppliers.

Despite the wide acceptance that appeals to localism have as a sustainability strategy, it is important to be careful when implementing this idea. The following discussion briefly reviews four issues that cast a shadow on the efficacy of the concept: the definition of what local actually means in practice, the ultimate effectiveness of localism, the challenges posed by the "local trap," and the charge that localist reforms are merely ameliorative rather than transformative.

First, even among locavores, there is no clear definition of what constitutes "local"; the concept is generally applied to suggest that a specific commodity or product originates from within an area that has political significance (for example, the state of Vermont in the United States) or a recognizable region (for example, Yorkshire in the United Kingdom). Since retailers often invoke the designation, it can also apply to a particular shopping district, even if most of the merchandise is from distant locales. Under such circumstances, localism becomes a source, simultaneously, of convenience and confusion – more a marketing enticement than a meaningful characterization.

Without a fixed and objective determination of how to assess localness, the idea becomes vague and poorly conceptualized. Making the problem more challenging is that relative degrees of local integrity are typically assessed in terms of measures like, for instance, "food miles" or "food kilometers" (to denote the distance that a product travels from farm to table). However, the amount of energy used to deliver an item varies based on the specific mode of transportation and numerous other factors. These considerations do not mean to suggest that local claims are disingenuous or duplicitous, or that they lack scientific foundation. It is, though, necessary to be attentive to the fact that invocations of "local" seek to reinforce certain economic interests even as they challenge others. Given that such claims are refracted by a political lens, the efficacy of local appeals need to be scrutinized.

Second, in some social networks, the performance of localist provisioning practices has become an increasingly important facet of individual identity formation and social communication. The emotional content of debates centering on these considerations can sometimes become quite intense and reach a point where the actual social and environmental dimensions drop out of view. The larger dilemma is that just because a product is sourced locally does not mean it has a sustainability profile that is superior to its alternatives. Some items are produced in certain areas – for instance, winter tomatoes in Sweden – because of large financial subsidies and inputs of energy. Just because they are locally cultivated does not necessarily make them in any way more sustainable. Swedish consumers interested in lowering the carbon footprint of their diet during out-of-season periods would do better to purchase Brazilian-grown varieties (or suspend their consumption of tomatoes for several months each year). The advantages of this alternative are borne out by the fact that transportation typically constitutes a relatively small part of overall energy inputs, and carbon emissions of most food products account for less than 20 percent of their total effects (Weber and Matthews 2008).

It also merits noting that, because of the significant environmental problems associated with meat and dairy production, a diet that includes sizable amounts of these items – even if they are locally produced – is likely to be less sustainable than one based on imported fruits and vegetables. However, it would be remiss to overlook the social benefits that oftentimes accrue when economic exchange takes place between neighbors as opposed to buyers and sellers separated by thousands of miles. Calibrating and contrasting these incommensurate outcomes poses methodological challenges and drives home the point that, while localism has heuristic value, it is not an entirely unambiguous way to guide decision-making.

What this all suggests is that localism is typically based on an extremely strategic and selective form of preference. As a practical matter, most locavores purchase goods from nearby sources when they are conveniently available and rely at other times on products arriving via long-distance supply chains. To do otherwise would entail, for a large majority of consumers, having to adapt to a much less diversified array of consumer goods. Concomitantly, localism is not a universally feasible strategy. What does a stringent emphasis on this mode of provisioning mean for regions that have poor endowments in terms of weather, soil conditions, energy availability, and so forth, and are unable to produce a varied assortment of goods? Is it sustainable to deny the residents of such places access to the same kinds of products that are available in temperate areas? This is actually just the tip of the iceberg in terms of the large number of questions about equitable impact that an emphasis on localism engenders.

A third problem for localism is, as mentioned above, that locavores presume that devolving responsibilities to more proximate scales necessarily leads to more effective and sustainable outcomes. Whether the issue is ensuring the wholesomeness of food supplies, protecting water resources, or generating energy, the supposition is that localization has the capacity to ensure more socially desirable and environmentally responsible results. It turns out that, on closer examination, the evidence is more mixed than proponents are typically prepared to acknowledge. Brown and Purcell (2005: 609), who term this the "local trap," observe:

> No scale has any inherent and eternal qualities that make it particularly suited to a specific social and ecological process ... [and] the characteristics of a given scale or scalar arrangement cannot be assumed a priori; rather the social and ecological outcomes of any particular scalar arrangement are the result of the political strategies of particular actors, not the inherent qualities of a particular scale.

The local trap arises from methodological confusion over means and ends. Locavores' commitment to more proximate systems of production and consumption is treated as an end-point objective, when in fact localism is a strategy – a means – for achieving a particular goal. It does not automatically lead to more sustainable outcomes. Local sourcing can, under certain circumstances, be a useful way to foster equity, food security, nutritional quality, and other constituent aims of sustainability, but there is no reason to suppose that these auspicious outcomes are automatically realizable. In fact, an emphasis on the local scale can just as readily lead to closed-mindedness, homogeneity, parochialism, exploitation, and xenophobia, as it can facilitate social and economic resilience and environmental responsibility. Other scholars push this critique further and contend that the turn toward local provisioning reinforces neoliberal prerogatives and instrumental dependency, rather than mutual support. In addition, it is alleged that the emphasis on individual responsibility and consumer sensibilities more deeply entrenches patterns of economic inequity, social injustice, and political inequality (Guthman 2008; Harris 2009).

Finally, some critics of localism are generally supportive of the premise, but regard the strategy as insufficiently radical and transformative, especially with respect to challenging – or even overturning – the organizational logic of capitalism. A robust presentation of this view is provided by activist and author Greg Sharzer (2012: 2) who writes:

> While small-scale alternatives can survive and occasionally flourish, they won't build a new, equitable society. Their prospects are severely limited by the power of capital. The problem with localism is not its anti-corporate politics, but that those politics don't go far enough. It sees the effects of unbridled competition but not is cause ... [I]f

localists had a greater understanding of how capitalism works, they might not be localists.

Furthermore, critics charge that localist initiatives will do little more than forge "tiny alternatives at the margins" because they sidestep the issue of class struggle and are less a political challenge to capitalism than a withdrawal from it. A still more piercing appraisal emerges out of the question of why poor people should be urged to grow their own food when they are already required to toil for substandard wages and to subject themselves to all manner of social indignities. Furthermore, localism, as noted above, is motivated by neoliberal commitments because it gives governments a free pass from having to address issues that contribute to poverty and diffuses pressure on capitalists to raise wages because the subsistence needs of workers are being ostensibly satisfied through alternative modes of provisioning.

There is insufficient space here to discuss the finer points of this set of perspectives, but suffice it to say that, while localism often has powerful appeal, it paints with a very broad brush. Although certainly not representative of all varieties, some localist initiatives do confront capitalist prerogatives, give participants opportunities to develop political organizing skills, provide alternative livelihoods, and serve as transferable and scalable modes of credible social change. Moreover, dismissing as misguided all reform strategies that are not committed to overturning capitalism is shortsighted and likely to resonate only with the most militant locavores. We should not underestimate the fact that certain expressions of localism create liminal spaces that serve as protected incubators for new ways of understanding and the routinization of novel social practices. In addition, the real world differs substantially from the theoretical formulations based on unbridled competition, perfect information, and so forth that inform the caricatured worldviews of not only economists, but also their most vociferous critics. We do better to rely more on empirical evidence and grounded insights pertaining to how people actually conduct themselves and pursue their ambitions than on ideological portrayals.

Lifestyle Minimalism

Critical appraisal of industrialism has included an emphasis on minimalist lifestyles going back at least to the mid-nineteenth century ascetic Henry David Thoreau, who for a time lived a semi-reclusive life on the shores of Walden Pond, not far from Concord, Massachusetts. An emphasis on frugality periodically emerged during the following decades – for example, in the formation of back-to-the-land movements, the establishment of religiously inspired retreats, the creation of countercultural communes, and the emergence of new aesthetic practices in art and design. During the 1980s and 1990s, "voluntary simplicity" developed as a loosely coordinated social movement that explored the relationship between avoidance of materialism, sustainability, and lifestyle satisfaction. Japanese traditional arts like *ikebana* (flower arranging) and *haiku* (short-form poetry), which embody ideas of transience and imperfection (referred to as *wabi-sabi*), have had an outsize influence on contemporary conceptions of lifestyle minimalism (Chinchilla and Luque 2019).

Sustainability practitioners interested in scaling back their material accumulations have incorporated these ideas of conscious restraint into various social experiments that avoid shopping, automobile use, air travel, or spending money on non-essential purchases. While it is important not to lose focus on the need for systemic change, efforts to lessen personal commitments to consumption can usefully enhance individual mindfulness. Furthermore, when pursued collectively by a group, such actions can contribute to shifts in habitual practices and cultural understanding. This section discusses three contemporary expressions of lifestyle minimalism: the systematic reduction of household possessions, the purposeful downsizing of residential space, and the purging of plastics from everyday living.

First, overaccumulation of possessions has become a societal phenomenon of increasing concern in recent decades. This situation arises from the fact that, in a consumer society, people are under continual, and oftentimes extreme, pressure to acquire goods, and when the rate of disposal fails to keep pace, various logistical and social problems tend to occur (Cohen 2017). Management of this dilemma has generated a sizable industry comprising commercial storage providers, customized closet designers, and professional home organizers. Especially notable in recent years has been the popularity of Japanese decluttering expert Marie Kondō, who has become an international celebrity through media appearances, books, and even a television series (see, for example, Kondō 2014). Her trademark advice involves encouraging devotees to ask themselves whether particular objects "spark joy" and to discard those items that fail this test.[7]

While it has not achieved the same popular notoriety or extensive reach as Marie Kondō and her hundreds of certified specialists (so-called KonMari consultants), the Swedish custom of *dostadning* (which translates into the "art of death cleaning") is another lifestyle philosophy for reducing the excessive accrual of stuff. The concept refers to a national tradition of clearing out unwanted household goods while one is still physically able in order to avoid eventually imposing the inconvenient task on family members or others. Enthusiasm for this idea beyond

Sweden has prompted publication of at least a half a dozen books and workbooks and numberless articles in magazines and online outlets (see, for example, Magnusson 2018).

These approaches have value as sustainability strategies to the extent that the undertakings that they induce are not just one-off interventions that simply set the stage for subsequent rounds of accumulation. The problem is that the authors of these decluttering manuals – and the fervent adherents who have been attracted to them – are mostly offering self-help advice rather than content that either facilitates understanding of the social and environmental implications of consumerist lifestyles or prompts appraisal of the relationship between materialism and the good life. The unfortunate and paradoxical effect is that an emphasis on minimalism ends up becoming just the latest marketing fad.

Second, from a sustainability standpoint, the dual processes of suburbanization and residential upsizing of the past several decades have been extremely problematic. According to the American Enterprise Institute, the average size of new houses built in the United States increased by more than 1,000 square feet between 1973 and 2015 (from 1,660 to 2,687).[8] Larger homes require more materials to construct and more energy to maintain. Compounding the situation is that this trend unfolded during a period of time when average household size was declining, thus amplifying the expansion in living space per person (Cohen 2020). The associated decline in population density has also increased the cost of providing public services and made it virtually impossible to avoid everyday reliance on a personal car.

There are indications that this pattern is now beginning to reverse. Notable numbers of Millennials (also known as Generation Y) demonstrate a preference for urban as opposed to suburban (or rural) lifestyles and are either reducing or giving up altogether on owning a car. Increasing numbers of people are not even bothering to get a driver's license – part of what transportation planners have described as "peak car." Related to these developments around mobility practices is a penchant for smaller-scale living. So-called micro-apartments of approximately 250–500 square feet are becoming fashionable residences in a growing number of cities (see Box 5.4). Other communities are encouraging the construction of "accessory dwelling units" (also known as "granny flats" or "mother-in-law apartments") which are either attached or detached residential accommodation co-located with a primary residence. Another case of residential downsizing with significant sustainability advantages involves the creation of dual co-living/co-working facilities that allow residents to live and work on the same premises.

Box 5.4: Microsized apartments

In a growing number of global cities with exorbitant prices for rental housing, microsized apartments are becoming a stylish residential option. The trend extends beyond Tokyo, Singapore, and London, which have long been at the top of international lists of urban areas with sky-high prices for small living spaces, and is evident in New York, San Francisco, Boston, and even the Detroit suburbs. Millennials and other young cosmopolitan professionals evince less interest in encumbering themselves with overly large spaces and are prepared to trade square footage for convenient access to valued amenities. Rather than confine themselves to a living area defined by four walls, these urbanites regard the city around them as an extension of their residence.

Micro-apartments are about 150–250 square feet (ft^2) (14–23 square meters (m^2)) in size and tend to be designed with raised ceilings and large windows to make the physical space seem roomier than it is. It is also common to create multifunctional areas and to outfit the living area with space-economizing furnishings such as hideaway beds, collapsible tables, and stackable chairs, as well as public areas for socializing and storage. Driving the trend are efforts by planners to create residential options that respond to new demographic realities: single-person households are the most rapidly expanding segment of the population in many cities. Another motivation is to reduce reliance on shared accommodation that can intensify gentrification in cases where three or four roommates working for, say, information-technology startups can oftentimes afford to pay more in rent than a modest-income family.

A pioneering project in the trend toward microsized apartments is Carmel Place (formerly known as My Micro NY) located in New York City. Conceived in 2012 as part of a design competition, the nine-story building comprises 55 rental units ranging in size from 260 ft^2 to 360 ft^2 (24–33 m^2). Of these, 14 are designated as affordable and 8 are reserved for formerly homeless veterans. Similar initiatives have sprung up in numerous other cities and become popular because of their cost, convenience, and efficiency. Residents especially value the services of the building's "community manager," who coordinates housekeeping and pet care and organizes movie nights and barbeques on the roof deck.

Source: "Microapartments": https://www.curbed.com/micro-apartments.

Finally, the problem of plastic waste has rapidly achieved public prominence in recent years. Driven by powerful media portrayals, social movement campaigns, and China's decision in 2017 to ban the import of recyclable materials, many consumers have developed newfound understanding of the massive amount of plastic that is produced – an estimated 380 million tons per year – with the vast majority of it discarded after a single use. In many countries, plastic waste washes down streams and rivers and the disused material becomes a source of ocean pollution, in some cases accumulating in gigantic subsurface cyclones like the North Pacific Garbage Patch discussed in Chapter 3, which science educator Marcus Eriksen and filmmaker Joel Paschal have described as a "toilet bowl that never flushes."[9]

Prompted by these circumstances, growing numbers of people have been motivated to reduce significantly their consumption of plastic packaging and some are even seeking to live completely plastic-free. Given the sheer quantity of consumer products that are distributed in plastic containers and wrapping, it might seem unrealistic that concerted action could make much of a dent in the overall problem. However, advocates contend that, like any bad habit, progress is best made one step at a time, first, for example, by banning plastic beverage bottles, then moving on to change the way in which other products are packaged, like milk, shampoo, laundry detergent, and so forth. Increasingly, glass, silicone, and cardboard alternatives are becoming available, as well as stores specializing in plastic-free goods and new closed-loop systems that enable the reuse of product packaging. In addition, local governments are expanding bans on plastic bags and instituting prohibitions on single-use plastics. For instance, Penzance, a coastal community in Cornwall, was in 2015 the first UK community to be certified as a "plastic-free" town, and just five years later more than 600 others had received this designation (Usborne 2018; Letcher 2020).

Livelihoods in the Era of Digital Automation

While sustainability specialists have long been attentive to changes in the organization of work, concerns about the rising tide of digital automation – and its risks in terms of economic security, social equity, and human health and the environment – has become a matter of increasing concern. Generally understood as encompassing applications in artificial intelligence, robotics, virtual reality, digital personal assistants, and automated vehicles, most assessments suggest that the deployment of these technologies will intensify in coming years and be a significant source of social and economic disruption. The dilemma – or perhaps the opportunity – is oftentimes expressed in terms of how to anticipate and plan for "the future of work." However, for current purposes, we can understand it in more expansive terms, namely as "the future of livelihoods." As discussed above with respect to the "sharing economy," a key source of concern is that, as customary wage-based employment becomes less readily available, and people become increasingly reliant on contingent and flexible forms of work (sometimes referred to as "gig jobs"), familiar modes of provisioning will lose their viability.

This book is not the place for a comprehensive appraisal of the forecasted timelines and trajectories of relevant digital automation technologies (see Brynfolfsson and McAfee 2014); the aim, instead, is to highlight issues that are paramount to shaping their societal dimensions in ways that could facilitate more sustainable outcomes. Accordingly, this section reviews three propositions that are currently attracting attention: reduced working hours, universal basic income, and business models predicated on mutualism and cooperation.

First, on initial blush, the notion of reducing working hours likely comes across as a peculiar way to decrease resource consumption and to curtail greenhouse-gas emissions, and it is perhaps still more puzzling as a strategy for narrowing income inequality. It is, though, an old idea and its pivotal significance stems from the need to offset improvements in labor efficiency and to achieve a more equitable distribution of available work. The British economist John Maynard Keynes argued in a renowned essay entitled "Economic Possibilities for our Grandchildren": "We are being afflicted with a new disease of which some readers may not yet have heard the name, but of which they will hear a great deal in the years to come – namely, *technological unemployment*. This means unemployment due to our discovery of means of economising the use of labour outrunning the pace at which we can find new uses for labour" (1963 [1930]: 364; italics in original). Keynes anticipated a day seven decades into the future when a 15-hour workweek would be the norm.

The upshot of Keynes's observation was that, due to technological change and other factors, advanced economies tend to achieve annual productivity improvements of approximately 2 percent. This means that with each passing year a national economy actually needs fewer working hours to generate the same volume of goods and services. However, as a matter of public policy what generally occurs is that productivity improvements are leveraged to expand production and to impel economic growth. This system condition creates the need to relentlessly increase consumption.

Degrowth proponents and other sustainability practitioners contend that, rather than stoking production and consumption year after year to offset productivity-induced unemployment, we should be taking advantage of these efficiency improvements to reduce working hours (Kallis et al. 2013; Pullinger 2014). They argue that a shift from a 40-hour to, say, a 25-hour workweek would enable a fairer allocation of available work while expanding the amount of time that each worker had to devote to leisure or other nonwork pursuits. At the same time, it is recognized that the second- and third-order effects of such a policy shift would be extremely complex. How will people reallocate their time under such circumstances? Is it possible to forecast the magnitude of anticipated reductions in resource utilization? What are the equity implications of sizeable changes in working hours across income cohorts? How will workers make up for the lost income? Most advocates concede that we do not know at present the answers to these questions – and likely numerous others. Rather, they contend that policymakers should devote the same consideration to them as they do to more customary technological options.

Urgency is compounded by the likelihood that the next generation of applications in digital automation will result in extremely significant gains in productivity. As tasks increasingly shift to artificial intelligence platforms, Siri-like devices, general-purpose robots, and autonomous vehicles, large numbers of people will be at risk of falling victim to, as Keynes described the problem, technological unemployment. Some forecasts anticipate that the next wave of transformative change will involve the "deindustrialization" of the service economy in advanced economies and "premature deindustrialization" across large parts of the developing world (Rodrik 2016). The loss of economic security and rise of precarious livelihoods in the face of a "jobless future" have the potential to compound current sustainability challenges in unprecedented ways. As historical evidence suggests, this process will probably proceed slowly, perhaps even for a considerable period, but will then reach a tipping point and occur very fast. Societal disruption on a mass scale can be expected to ensue in the absence of adequate preparation.

Second, a related strategy to reduce the likelihood of significant privation as digital automation becomes more pervasive is to implement a universal basic income (UBI, also referred to as a guaranteed annual income or citizen's basic income). A UBI would provide households with an assured monthly payment to compensate partly for the loss of earnings from salaried employment. There are numerous details about the design of specific programs that policymakers would need to work out, but the general thrust of the idea calls for a disbursement regardless of age, wealth, or other sociodemographic factors. The commitment to universality is important because it is a way to avoid the stigma associated with conventional forms of social welfare and to reduce the administrative expenses of having to enforce cumbersome eligibility requirements. Contemporary expressions of the concept date back to the 1960s and 1970s when places as seemingly dissimilar as New Jersey and Manitoba launched some of the first experiments to test the idea (Boeckmann 1976; Calnitsky 2016).

Recent years have seen a host of initiatives to test the viability of a UBI. Finland implemented an experiment that distributed €560–2,000 to randomly selected and unemployed citizens in 2017 and 2018. Other countries, including Kenya, Uganda, and Namibia, have introduced their own pilots, and numerous cities around the world – from Newark, New Jersey, to Glasgow, Scotland – have recently created taskforces to investigate the feasibility of the concept.

Though it is not always immediately obvious as a UBI program, the Alaska Permanent Fund (APF), established in 1980 and financed by a tax on oil production, offers an interesting model. A portion of the revenue is retained by the state for investment and the remaining share is dispensed as an annual divided to every resident (generally amounting to between $1,000 and $2,000 per person). Several other resource-dependent nations and regions maintain pension funds, sovereign wealth funds, and other similar financial arrangements that function in practical terms as UBIs. Various proposals have been advanced for cap-and-dividend programs (that reallocate the proceeds of carbon permits in the form of a "citizen's dividend" to lower-income households) and common-asset trusts (that impose fees for the appropriation of natural resources and return a portion to the public as a periodic payout).

Finally, the coming wave of digital automation may provide an opportune time to consider how prevalent business models, overwhelmingly predicated on the maximization of shareholder value, oftentimes frustrate prospects for sustainability transitions. There are numerous organizational forms premised on cooperative ownership that, with the exception of a few geographic regions and industrial sectors, have been generally relegated to marginal status. Further exacerbating the situation is that within the community of mutually operated businesses there is a kind of Iron Curtain between worker and consumer cooperatives.

The need to avert the disruption that is likely forthcoming in the wake of widespread arrival of the robots and their allied technologies provides an opportunity to attenuate customary modes of shareholder ownership and to rethink the role of cooperativism. A useful source of inspiration is the Eroski Supermarket Group (part of the venerable Mondragón Corporation) headquartered in the Basque region of Spain. The company operates several hundred supermarkets and hypermarkets, as well as a variety of other retail businesses, across the country. After a series of economic crises during the 1970s, Eroski reorganized itself into a hybrid worker-consumer (also termed a multistakeholder) cooperative, meaning that all its employees and customers are co-owners of the company. Rather than sending the profits to shareholders, who have no interest in the affairs of the business beyond the size of their dividend or rise in the stock price, Eroski exists to enhance the livelihoods of the more than 30,000 people who have an enduring stake in its performance (see Box 5.5).

Box 5.5: Weaver Street Market

Weaver Street Market is a modestly sized hybrid worker-consumer cooperative specializing in natural foods located in the Research Triangle Park area of North Carolina in the United States. The first store opened in 1988 in the town of Carrboro, with initial funding provided by a local credit union, the municipal government, and a combination of individual loans and shareholder equity. In subsequent years, the company opened three additional shops in the region (Hillsborough, Southern Village, and Raleigh) as well as a food-preparation facility. Ownership of Weaver Street Market is in the hands of 200 workers and 18,000 customer-households.

Since its inception, the co-op has sought to be more than simply a supermarket selling healthy food and has developed a deeply rooted commitment to social enterprise. Over the years, it has established a housing cooperative, a community-owned radio station, and a charitable fund. Weaver Street Market's mission statement emphasizes ten principles: cooperative control of profits, local self-reliance, ecological balance, meeting basic community needs, non-exploitation of the workforce, inclusiveness of the community, education of fellow citizens, social interactivity, empowerment of customers, and integration in the local economy. The co-op has been a leader in local sourcing and fair trade and stresses the importance of "authentic food," defined as:

> Organic products from small farms that embody the spirit of organic farming rather than factory farms that do the minimum to get by. Authentic food means products from local producers who contribute to a sustainable food system, retain artisan production techniques, and allow family farmers to stay in business. Authentic food means fair trade – fair payment to farmers in the developing world that produce crops such as coffee that can only be grown in warmer climates. Authentic food means products from our own kitchen and bakery, where we use high quality ingredients and maximize quality and freshness.

Yes! Magazine recognized Weaver Street Market as one of the best alternative businesses in the country; it serves as a model for other cooperative businesses looking to be engines of progressive social change in their communities.

Source: Weaver Street Market: https://www.weaverstreetmarket.coop. Michael Schuman, Alissa Barron, and Wendy Wasserman, *Community Food Enterprise: Local Success in a Global Marketplace.* Arlington, VA: Wallace Center at Winrock International and the Business Alliance for Local Living Economies, 2009: https://archive.org/stream/fp_Weaver_Street_Market_Co-operative-Case_Study/Weaver_Street_Market_Co-operative-Case_Study_djvu.txt.

While we should not underestimate the obstacles to creating multi-stakeholder cooperatives on a meaningful scale, it merits noting that research suggests these business models have the potential to foster communal goodwill and other-regarding dispositions. Participation in organizations of the kind described above could be a useful way to enhance social cohesion while more adequately meeting essential needs. Though we must regard the claim as provisional at this point, this kind of engagement could be a useful way of safeguarding households during a period of heightened vulnerability arising from large-scale transformational change. At the same time, it is necessary to keep in mind the challenges that will need to be overcome in terms of organizational fragility, limited access to capital, and hurdles recruiting appropriate forms of institutional sponsorship.

Conclusion

The prevailing tendency is to regard sustainability as a grand idea for surmounting a growing accumulation of environmental challenges, the most salient of which is climate change. For some people, interrelated issues pertaining to inequality and equity are an important part of the discussion, but it is extremely rare to encounter propositions that adopt a fully integrated view and still more exceptional for policymakers to advance strategies formulated in accordance with a full spectrum understanding in mind. To compensate for this imbalance, this chapter asserts that sustainability is primarily a social problem and we should be wary of the ultimate effectiveness of purely technological proposals.

Unfortunately, we face a still more difficult dilemma. Several of the most popular social innovations these days – sharing and collaborative consumption, self- and communal provisioning, economic localization, and minimalist lifestyles – are not as straightforward as many of their most ardent proponents contend. We need to apply these recommendations carefully if they are going to provide efficacious pathways. In addition, human capabilities are evolving rapidly and there is every reason to expect that customary livelihoods will be upended in coming years because of advances in digital automation that vastly reduce the need for labor. Passionate debates are currently occurring between, on the one hand, visionaries who contend that there is little reason for concern (we have thrived from prior waves of inventive disruption), and, on the other, pragmatists, who urge caution and restraint (there are indications that the emergent situation could be without precedent).

It is foolhardy to contend that we can predict the future with any reliability. It is equally inadvisable to bury our heads in the sand. While defenders of the status quo often disparage sustainability for promoting an emphasis on stasis, this is a cynical and misleading caricature. Sustainability practitioners are not seeking to put society under glass or to achieve some kind of eternal and perpetuating natural balance. They are instead continually scanning the horizon for unfolding developments, those that offer promise of enhancing the human condition and others that suggest pending hazards or otherwise threaten to undermine our well-being. At the same time, some prescient observers are speculating that it may be time to consider new or previously overlooked conceptual frameworks. We take up these perspectives in the next chapter of this book.

6

Toward
Post-Sustainability?

Introduction

A key proposition of this book has been that innovation – to differing degrees both technological and social – has an important role to play in a prospective sustainability transition. At the same time, it is understandable if readers maintain a certain lack of clarity about what might constitute a successful transformation. Indeed, among sustainability scientists and practitioners, there are different interpretations about how such a process might unfold and, to date, only limited progress in dealing with the challenge that sustainability is, as described in Chapter 1, an essentially contested concept.

While this ambiguity has been a source of important advantage from the standpoint of political discourse, it has simultaneously led to the proliferation of an uncontainable jumble of competing, and at times spurious, formulations. We have conceptions narrowly premised on "environmental" or "eco-" sustainability that seek to sever and isolate certain biophysical aspects from their arguably inseparable social dimensions. The situation is even more confounding when the notion of "greening" is invoked as a quasi-synonym for sustainability. This nuanced substitution opens the door to a host of permissive and hazily defined initiatives centered on, for instance, "green buildings," "green cars," and apparently limitless numbers of "green consumer goods."

Such claims are typically deployed more to create misunderstanding and to seize market advantage than to offer alternatives that will credibly reduce energy and material throughput on the Earth system and enhance social equity and inclusion (Kaufman 2009). Policymakers unfortunately are often complicit in these transgressions because they calibrate their proposals to secure quick political "wins" to assuage fleeting public concerns rather than to set the stage for cumulating and durable progressive change.

Under such circumstances, the pursuit of sustainability is often confined to "techno-fix" interventions that are only able to provide ameliorative correctives to environmentally problematic and socially unjust practices. This is not necessarily a new development. The historical record provides recurrent evidence demonstrating how these "solutions," because they are conceived in overly narrow terms and fail to recognize that technologies are ultimately embedded in societal contexts, have a tendency to ramify in unexpected ways and to spark unintended secondary consequences (Rees 2009; Levidow and Paul 2011). Less technology-reliant initiatives, such as the examples discussed in Chapter 5, are typically limited to small-scale experiments and dismissed as impractical for widespread adoption. Faced with such a situation in which sustainability has been either weakened to the edge of impotence or hijacked by guardians of the status quo, it is understandable why many conscientious people are dismayed. Some of them even fall victim to a kind of fatalistic catastrophism and this particular reaction has, in recent years, become a notable feature of popular culture (Vogelaar et al. 2018). Even more alarming is that mental health clinicians and others report a rising incidence of trauma attributable to policy failures to address climate change and other sustainability challenges (Whitmee et al. 2015).

It is perhaps then unsurprising that a growing list of commentators has begun to suggest that after three decades of increasing prominence sustainability has reached its end (see, for example, Robinson 2012; Foster 2017a, 2017b; Sconfienza 2019). Like a ship picking up passengers at a sequence of ports, the promise of a more sustainable future has collected over the years a multifarious array of issues and aspirations. However, bickering among the travelers has caused the captain to become distracted and to lose his sense of direction. This concluding chapter begins by repeating some of the early concerns of close observers of sustainability and contends that the lack of unambiguous achievements is due to the problematic way in which the voyage was initially planned. The current situation has led some analysts to propose replacement of both ship and skipper and – hopefully – to bring an agreeable destination back into view. A range of ideas has emerged, and the discussion below provides broad outlines of six propositions. The conclusion strives to identify some common themes and to ensure that our vessel is seaworthy for the next phase of the journey.

Did Sustainability Set Off with the Wrong Navigational Plan?

Some commentators have alleged that sustainability was destined to lose its way because its initial navigational plan – namely the Brundtland Report released in 1987 – was inadequately prepared. As environmental sociologist Michael Redclift (1991) noted at the time, the notion of "sustainable development" was conceived to dampen and reorient insurgent forms of environmentalism that by the 1980s had coalesced into visionary programs of societal reform (see also Redclift 1987). Pointing specifically to radical ecology, ecofeminism, and deep ecology, he asserted that these political movements rejected "technical solutions to environmental problems" and regarded them as "ultimately self-defeating." In addition, the Brundtland Report was fraught with compromises intended to narrow the postcolonial divide between so-called developed and developing countries. As Redclift observed (1991: 38): "In the South struggles over the environment are usually about basic needs, [and] strategies to survive ... [T]here is no point in appealing, under these circumstances, to idealism or altruism to protect the environment, when the individual and household are forced to behave 'selfishly' in their struggle to survive." By contrast, he argued that sustainability issues in the North were premised on "lifestyles" and these concerns "can often be inverted in the South, where the environment is contested not because it is valued in itself, but because its destruction creates value." Perhaps most fatal, though, from Redclift's perspective was the failure of the Brundtland Report to seriously engage with "the contradictions imposed by the structural inequalities of the global system."

Another prescient observer at the time was environmental philosopher Dale Jamieson, who argued that that these inconsistencies were ultimately responsible for the displacement of "sustainable development" with "sustainability." He asserted that the global North was never very interested in development per se and truncating the concept enabled "the colonization of the sustainable development discourse by economists" (1988: 184). Jamieson proceeded to observe that sustainability had become "primarily an economistic and anthropocentric notion" and the "moral reorientation that is required, which involves new relationships between humans as well as with other animals and the rest of nature, is unlikely to be affected by developing ever more precise understandings of sustainability. We need a discourse that permits deeper discussion of aesthetic, spiritual, religious, cultural, political, and moral values" (1998: 191).

It is precisely these questions pertaining to how humanity should adapt itself to the constraints imposed by the Earth system that became marginalized in favor of an emphasis on managing natural resources to ensure continued economic growth through improvements in techno-logical efficiency. As for issues of equity and political participation, they were largely dropped from mainstream consideration, a situation that prompted environmental sociologist Magnus Boström (2012) to describe them as the "missing pillar" of sustainability. Though traced out here only in a thumbnail manner, this recapitulation reminds us of how sustainability came to be subsumed by political agendas for encouraging "green growth" and building a "green economy" despite an absence of evidence that these ambitions could realistically be achieved on a global scale. Nonetheless, we find ourselves in the unfortunate situation where there exists a widespread impression that by being better shoppers we can achieve societal changes that offer a modicum of sustainability.

A further line of critique is that early proponents of sustainability, notwithstanding their hopefulness and good intentions, made two tragic errors. In the first instance, they underestimated the capacity of capitalism to appropriate and reframe initial aspirations. The expec-tation was that economic institutions would adapt themselves to the requirements of a less resource-intensive and socially inequitable future. In fact, as discussed in Chapter 3, there were notable efforts on the part of prominent multinational corporations during the 1990s to implement new auditing systems and to improve certain aspects of their operations in accordance with sustainability performance criteria. However, they pursued these initiatives in the context of continued prioritization of increasing returns to shareholders and economic growth. Evidence of the weakness of this resolve became patently apparent during and after the Great Recession that began in 2007 (Geels 2013; Antal and Van Den Bergh 2013).

A second miscalculation derives from overconfidence in the influence of dominant governance institutions, particularly at national and global levels. Virtually across the board, sustainability indicators have continued to move since the early 1990s in the wrong direction, with perhaps the direst consequences evident with respect to climate change. The laudable, but regrettably insufficient, targets set by the 2016 Paris Agreement are proving to be mostly empty promises given the duplicity of national governments and the inherent weakness of international organizations. Because of these combined failures, according to scientific analysis conducted by Climate Action Tracker, the planet is currently on course to a 3°C increase in temperature by 2100.[1] More broadly, the SDGs represent a commendable effort to improve livelihoods around the world, but progress has been for the most part unsatisfactory. Reports prepared for the High-Level Political Forum on Sustainable Development held in 2019 observed that, "despite progress in a number of areas over the past four years, on some of the Goals, progress has been slow or even reversed. The most vulnerable people and countries continue to suffer the most and the global response has not been ambitious enough" (UNDESA 2019).

A discerning voice on the current travails of sustainability is philosopher John Foster, who characterizes the extant situation as a "paradigm failure." He notes:

> It is no longer completely out of court for thinkers and scholars concerned with environmental issues to argue that the "sustainability" discourse and policy paradigm have failed, and that we are moving into a new and much bleaker era. ... The argument is beginning to gain traction, then, that turning [sustainability] ... into a set of policy options represents a strategy which has had a good run for its money since the 1980s, but should now be recognized as well past its use-by date. (2017a: 1; see also Foster 2014, 2017b)

Expanding on this argument, a meta-analysis by Howes et al. (2017) examined nearly 100 published accounts of "policy failure" involving projects to advance environmental sustainability and, echoing much of the discussion above, found that the lack of success was attributable to a combination of structural causes, implementation traps, and knowledge-scoping deficiencies. More specifically, disappointment was largely due to continued reliance on perverse economic incentives, incapacity or insufficient political will on the part of governance institutions, and inadequate communication strategies. The authors conclude that "[t]hese three factors are mutually reinforcing" and indicate "a failure to convince decision-makers in all sectors that sustainable development offers a realistic pathway to a prosperous economy, a better society, and a healthy environment" (2017: 11).

Alternative Paradigms Beyond Sustainability

It is important to acknowledge that the above assertions are not advanced by critics who are unsympathetic to the normative dimensions of sustainability. While perhaps difficult for some readers to concede, the general argument deserves serious consideration. In fact, the timeliness of these allegations is prompting a growing number of sustainability specialists to reflect on whether the current paradigm has reached its limits and now needs to be replaced. Environmental activist and author Bill McKibben describes the scale of the predicament in his inimitably poetic style when he summons into existence the planet Eaarth (purposefully spelled with a double "a"). He writes:

> The planet on which our civilization evolved no longer exists. The stability that produced that civilization has vanished; epic changes have begun. ... We *may*, with commitment and luck, yet be able to maintain a planet that will sustain *some kind* of civilization, but it won't be the same planet, and hence it can't be the same civilization. The earth that we knew – the only earth that we ever knew – is gone. (2010: 27; italics in original)

If we accept McKibben's account, it is unlikely that current conceptions of sustainability are going to provide much in the way of credible assistance going forward. In light of these circumstances, this section summarizes several ideas that could serve as potential post-sustainability alternatives. These options are resilience, regenerative development/ design, coevolutionary revisioning, sustainability as flourishing, mobilization of a global citizens movement, and models for the next system. The ordering of the presentation is, roughly speaking, in accordance with the level of ambitiousness inherent in the respective frameworks, though it merits noting that no single paradigm is necessarily exclusive and the future *could* unfold in ways that combine elements of multiple perspectives.

Resilience

Initially conceived by ecologist C. S. (Buzz) Holling, the notion of resilience has become a familiar and established concept in the field of systems ecology and is defined as "the capacity of a system to absorb disturbance and reorganize while undergoing change so as to still retain essentially the same function, structure, identity, and feedbacks" (Walker et al. 2004). Also relevant has been the work of Nobel laureate Elinor Ostrom (2009), who applied the idea to the self-organizing capacities of social-ecological systems. An important source for moving the concept into wider prominence (including among sustainability scientists) was the popular book *Resilience: Why Things Bounce Back* by Andrew Zolli and Ann Marie Healy (2012). In subsequent commentary during the aftermath of a protracted summer heatwave and an extremely damaging hurricane-like "superstorm" on the east coast of the United States, Zolli (2012) explained "resilience thinking" as a strategy "to help vulnerable people,

organizations and systems persist, perhaps even thrive, amid unfore-
seeable disruptions. Where sustainability aims to put the world back into
balance, resilience looks for ways to manage in an imbalanced world."

The similarity and overlap between the two paradigms, given their
common pedigrees in the study of ecology, is probably not surprising and,
indeed, resilience shares many conceptual elements with sustainability-
oriented modes of land-use planning (such as relocating communities
from flood-prone areas). A recent bibliometric study by Marchese et al.
(2018) revealed the existence of three relational frameworks: resilience
as a component of sustainability, sustainability as a component of resilience, and resilience and sustainability as separate objectives.

Some resilience advocates have sought in recent years to build on the
separateness framework and to suggest that creating adaptive capacity
for resilience is fundamentally a different enterprise from that of
advancing sustainability. A prominent example is the work of geographer
Melinda Benson and legal scholar Robin Craig, who argue for the need
to renounce sustainability in favor of a new adherence to resilience. They
contend in a defiant article entitled "The End of Sustainability" that in
the Anthropocene there is "an urgent need to move past our current state
of denial" and "[f]rom a policy perspective, we must face the impos-
sibility of even defining – let alone pursuing – a goal of 'sustainability'
in a world characterized by extreme complexity, radical uncertainty,
and unprecedented change ... This adherence to sustainability ignores
the fact that the concept has failed to meaningfully change the human
behavior that created the Anthropocene" (2014: 778).

While they maintain general support for the goals of sustainability,
Benson and Craig argue that resilience provides a more effective
approach for governance, especially given the inevitable exigencies
and managerial complexities unleashed by climate change. From their
vantage point, the two primary conceits of sustainability moving forward
are that we know what can be sustained and that we have the capacity
to maintain a stationary state.[2] Resilience, by contrast, seeks to ensure
flexibility and adaptability to changing conditions based on capacities
for self-organization and learning. Anticipating the critical response that
this conception of resilience is prone to evoke, Benson and Craig (2014:
780) assert that "[s]hifting the governance focus from sustainability
to resilience is not admitting defeat ... [rather] a resilience approach
would reorient current research and policy efforts toward coping with
change instead of increasingly futile efforts to maintain existing states
of being." They further argue that resilience thinking is likely to offer
greater transparency with respect to social justice because the concept
explicitly considers how values are reflected in the policy decisions of
socioecological systems.

Regenerative development

The history of regenerative development (also termed regenerative design or regenerative sustainability) is exceedingly complex and interwoven with a number of influences.[3] Some scholars trace its initial philosophy and practical applications to the concept of permaculture (permanent agriculture), which developed during the 1970s and is predicated on the idea that cultivation should be restorative in the sense of renewing and enhancing the socioecological conditions in which cultivation occurs (Rhodes 2015). Another source of inspiration is the notion of bioregionalism which seeks to align human development in accordance with natural boundaries and potentialities, for example at the scale of a watershed (Sale 1985; McGinnis 1998; Glotfelty and Quesnel 2014).

Its essential ideas coevolved in subsequent decades with other system-oriented fields discussed throughout this book, including biomimicry, industrial ecology, ecological economics, ecological engineering, community development, and place-based design. Regenerative development also absorbed practices that were first trialed in countercultural social movements organized around appropriate technology, ecological design, renewable energy, natural building materials, and sufficient lifestyles. Particularly prominent wellsprings were Buckminster Fuller's system theory and architectural innovations, Edward Goldsmith's *Blueprint for Survival*, Ian McHarg's *Design with Nature*, Barry Commoner's *The Closing Circle*, E. F. Schumacher's *Small Is Beautiful*, Stewart Brand's *Whole Earth Catalog*, John Lyle's *Regenerative Design for Sustainable Development*, and David Orr's extensive writings and projects (Zelov and Cousineau 1997; Kirk 2007).

As discussed in Chapter 1, many of these same influences were essential in establishing the foundations of sustainable development during the 1970s and 1980s, but were then mostly set aside in favor of the techno-economic paradigm that came to characterize mainstream conceptions of sustainability. However, the ideas did not entirely disappear and some scholars and practitioners who have remained active at the fringes of the field carried on to further elaborate and test these concepts to a point at which they fused into the paradigm of regenerative development. This approach constitutes a worldview that aims to transcend mechanistic and reductionistic thinking. Architect Chrisna du Plessis (2012: 15) describes it as representing "a shift from seeing the planet as a deterministic clockwork system in which humans are separate from nature to seeing it as a fundamentally interconnected, complex, living and adaptive social-ecological system that is constantly in flux. In this system, humans are seen as an integral part of nature and partners in the processes of co-creation and co-evolution instead of being merely users or clients of various ecosystem services."

Du Plessis identifies three fundamental principles of regenerative development. First, human developmental efforts should be aligned with the creative capacity of natural systems. Second, episodic change is an essential and underlying condition, and human developmental efforts should focus on enhancing capabilities for effective adaptation and maintaining functional identity when confronted by disturbance. Finally, people and their artifacts are not separate and apart from nature, but, rather, are an inherent part of it. As such, human developmental efforts should be net positive (benefits in excess of harms) and contribute to processes of ongoing revitalization of the overall system.

Regenerative development is gaining increasing visibility and its principles are being applied in numerous areas, including agriculture, transportation, manufacturing, and urban planning. A particularly noteworthy context has been the design and construction of the built environment. According to environmental engineer and architect Raymond Cole (2012a: 3), the whole systems mode of practice that informs regenerative development differs from customary approaches to green design and shifts emphasis away from "doing less harm" to a "positive message of considering the act of building as one that can give back more than it receives and thereby over time [build] social capital." He continues by observing that designers working from this perspective need to prioritize *place* rather than *space*. This means training oneself to be attentive to the constraints and opportunities afforded by social and environmental endowments and "to developing communities integrated with their surrounding ecosystems." Acquiring this understanding typically entails processes of deep engagement and extensive partici- patory collaboration with a wide range of stakeholders, many of whom possess tacit knowledge that is integral to success.

Initiatives to implement regenerative development have also been launched at the municipal scale. A particularly notable example is the Oberlin Project in the small city with the same name in northeastern Ohio.[4] The current population of approximately 8,200 people has experi- enced in recent decades a familiar pattern of deindustrialization, and the community is primarily known today as the home of Oberlin College, a selective liberal arts institution with a time-honored commitment to progressive social change. Environmental educator David Orr, an early proponent of the project, describes it as an example of "full spectrum sustainability" (Orr 2015; see also Rosenberg Daneri et al. 2015; Jones 2017). He defines this concept as

neither a more clever way of doing the same old things nor is it tinkering with the coefficients of change. It is, rather, a change in the

structure of the systems that have rendered our future precarious ...
[It] requires that we learn to see the world – and ourselves – whole,
and apply intelligence, foresight, generosity of spirit, and civic compe-
tence to avoid unsolvable dilemmas and solve problems before they
become full-blown crises.

Orr explains the Oberlin Project as:

something like a jailbreak from the conventional silos, boundaries,
pigeonholes, disciplines, and bureaucracies by which we have organized
governments, economies, education, social movements, and entire
worldviews. It is an attempt to "connect the dots" between the various
parts of sustainability and thereby give form and operational vitality
to the word "systems" in the public realm, and to extend the time
horizon by which we judge our successes and failures and our profits
and losses ... [W]e assume that systemic failures that have led us to the
present crisis will require systems-level responses, smarter policies, and
alert citizens acting with foresight and civic acumen.

The practical elements of the project entail development of a downtown
green arts district; creation of new renewable-energy businesses; establishment of a local food economy; formation of a regional alliance of
several educational institutions; expansion of the dialogue to include
all of the humanities, the arts, the sciences, and the social sciences; and
collaboration with other stakeholders and communities. The Oberlin
Project is purposefully conceived as a long-term undertaking to develop
local capabilities to enable participants to respond to an uncertain future
buffeted by climate change and other sources of social and environmental disruption. Orr ultimately sees the initiative as "an exercise in
applied hope based on a commitment to make the world more fair and
decent while preserving a beautiful and livable Earth. And if we don't
stand for such things, what do we stand for?"

Coevolutionary revisioning

Formulated by environmentalist and ecological economist Richard
Norgaard (1994, 1995) coevolutionary revisioning is an expansive
framework for reinterpreting the seriousness of our contemporary social
and environmental predicament. The conception begins with acknowl-
edgement of our tendency to interpret the environmental crisis in material
terms – abundance of waste in the present and insufficient resources in
the future. Accordingly, when we search for ways to ameliorate these
conditions, we reflexively turn toward solutions predicated on new

technologies and more accurate price signals (generally through the imposition of taxes). This emphasis stems from a prevalent worldview in affluent nations that relies on materialist explanations to interpret the world around us. The dominance of this mode of thinking traces back to the sixteenth century and the rise of science – including diffusion of the idea of progress – as an epistemology to supplant religious understanding. As Norgaard (1995: 478) puts it, "[T]he idea that humanity was in an unending downward spiral by moral damnation was replaced by a positive, uplifting sense of both material and moral destiny, driven by science, that has been central to the identity of Western and westernized peoples to this day." While unquestionably beneficial in many respects, this shift stripped societies of any moral direction and assigned divine status to science (and the technological artifacts that it enabled). It also set people free from networks of communal reliance and solidarity.

Materialism led then to *positivism* (devotion to the validation of knowledge through empirical tests), *atomism* (the contention that phenomena are separable into ever smaller parts), *mechanism* (the view that the world is comprised of explicitly manageable and controllable parts), *universalism* (the idea that local variation can be subsumed by generalizable rules), and *economism* (the outlook that unhindered market transactions enable optimal allocation of resources). These interlocking developments significantly diminished the role of moral guidance of the common good in decision-making. Benchmarks as to what might constitute individually or societally sufficient levels of material accumulation disappeared, and satisfaction came to be measured in terms of the volume and novelty of purchasable goods that could be amassed.

The notion of coevolutionary revisioning posits that to make meaningful headway on our contemporary sustainability challenges, we need not only to reduce our materialist commitments, but also to formulate alternative cosmologies. But where to begin? As a start, Norgaard makes three observations.

First, the notion of communicative rationality developed by social philosopher Jürgen Habermas is insightful for its emphasis on the essential unity of parts of a system, namely that changes experienced by one element have ramifying effects on other elements. By extension, as Norgaard (1995: 486) expresses it, "[t]he words we use to describe the parts also do not stand alone but are constantly evolving new meaning as we try to understand changing parts and relations, communicate with each other, and, in effect, try to replicate the evolving cosmology in our own evolving discursive, collective understanding." This complication is compounded by the fact that we are ourselves inside the system so are ultimately unable to achieve the objective detachment that positivist science presumes is at our disposal. In other words, "[w]e cannot stand apart from the world and look at or understand it objectively because how we have looked at and understood it in the past affect how it is today" (1995: 486–7).

Second, if the parts of a system are continually coevolving, capacity for predication and control becomes extremely limited. Under these circumstances, resisting change stemming from innovation or seeking to manage disruption is likely to be futile. Rather, "maintaining diversity to keep options open, monitoring the changes, and adapting in order to 'go with flow' are the best we can do" (Norgaard 1995: 487). Expressed more optimistically, realization that we are part of the system, and coevolving with it, may help us to understand the origins of our sustainability challenges.

Finally, a coevolutionary framework reveals that rather than mutually adapting with the biophysical environment as was earlier the case, humans have become entwined with a fossil-fuel economy. Current livelihoods (at least in the high consuming countries) were enabled and facilitated, initially, by coal and, latterly, by oil and natural gas. Most contemporary sustainability challenges stem either directly or indirectly from our reliance on these energy sources. Because we have become alienated from the biophysical environment and have instead been coevolving with fossil fuels, we have lost our connections to nature. According to Norgaard (1995: 480), "[i]ll-fitting ideas about nature were no longer being selected out ... and [r]ather, we coevolved a whole system of values, institutions, and technologies around understandings which did not have to square with nature in the short run." We now find ourselves caught in a deeply problematic mismatch. To resolve this situation, we will need to sever our connection to fossil fuels and re-embed ourselves in nature. The philosophy of deep ecology arguably provides one way to achieve the required "revitalization of social communication that matches the complexity and depth of our relations with nature" (1995: 489).[5]

Sustainability as flourishing

Nobel laureate and economic philosopher Amartya Sen has championed the idea that human development should focus on enabling the capabilities of people to achieve individual freedom. Importantly, his understanding is not simply concerned with rights that may exist in a formal sense but, rather, how they are exercised given the existence of political disempowerment, economic marginalization, and other adverse circumstances.

In other words, Sen is interested in how freedom is experienced in the context of actual lived experience and a critical element of his so-called Capabilities Approach is that development is most vitally about capacity for human flourishing (see, for example, Sen 1999).[6] Environmental educator and author John Ehrenfeld takes this notion of flourishing as his point of departure for articulating a new paradigm of sustainability.

Ehrenfeld's conception begins by noting that conventional under-standing of sustainability is deficient because the concept itself is "fuzzy" and "complex" (2008: 48) and we have failed to construct an adequate definition or explain what exactly is meant to be sustained. Rather than adopt the managerialist interpretation deployed by the Brundtland Report, Ehrenfeld redefines sustainability as "the *possibility* that humans and other life will *flourish* on the Earth *forever*" (2008: 49; italics in the original). But what does it mean to flourish and how might such an ornate metaphor contribute to improvements in a world wracked by climate change, biodiversity loss, social inequality, and other sustain-ability challenges? Ehrenfeld elaborates by explaining each of the three italicized words in turn.

First, *possibility* is about a search for a better life and "enables humans to visualize and strive for a future that neither is available in the present nor may have existed in the past" (2008: 49). It provides a window through which we can transcend the travails of prior experi-ences and move toward an unhindered future. Ehrenfeld stresses that possibility should not be confused with probability because, in the latter case, the future is inevitably contingent on the present and his intent is to suggest that "[t]he future as possibility arises and transforms your Being now. Aliveness shows up when future is a possibility coming from nothingness. And what is a better image of being alive than flourishing?" (2008: 50).

Second, a *flourishing* life is an eternal idea and all cultures across the span of time have sought to give expression to its pursuit:

> Flourishing is behind the acts and lives of great leaders like Gandhi, King, and Mandela. Flourishing is in the poetry of William Blake and e. e. cummings. It appears every time an infant first smiles. It unfolds in the blooming of a rose. It comes in the taste of water from a country spring or after a deep breath in the forest. All humans have had at least a moment when their senses revealed flourishing, but all too few live in circumstances where those precarious moments reemerge over and over. (2008: 50)

Expressed in practical terms and borrowing partly from Sen's Capabilities Approach, Ehrenfeld identifies dignity as a cornerstone of flourishing. It is also predicated on justice, fairness, and equity. Flourishing additionally includes "a social dimension to living that recognizes in some way that all humans are interconnected and that the state of our individual lives is tied to the states of others with whom we share our only world" (2008: 51). Beyond these essential characteristics, Ehrenfeld contends that it is not easy to elaborate on the individual elements that might further round out a more elaborate definition. Part of this difficulty is due to the fact that flourishing "is technically an emergent property of a complex living system ... [and] [s]uch properties, like beauty, always emerge within the context of the observers or actors in the system and take on characteristics determined by that context" (2008: 52). In other words, flourishing is not something that exists on its own, but becomes manifest as a function of the relationships inherent in the system that produces it. This condition leads to an extremely exigent situation from the standpoint of policy and practice, namely that properties like flourishing are not measurable in any conventional sense.

Finally, assertion of a commitment to *forever* brings the definition into alignment with most contemporary understandings of sustainability. Implicit in contemporary usage of the term is that activities in the present will not diminish the prospects of the next generation and so on into infinitude – a guideline that, however desirable, raises questions in terms of physical laws. Ehrenfeld seeks to make a more pragmatic point and to convey the need to consider the consequences of current actions on future opportunities "in a meaningful way beyond the mere discounting of some economic calculus" (2008: 53).

The intention is to foster a new vision of sustainability, one that is not instrumentally centered on means and ends. Ehrenfeld poses the question:

> Doesn't this way of speaking raise a very different image and feeling from the notion of sustainable development? It doesn't say much about how to get there and it doesn't say how we will ever know whether we are indeed there. Sustainability is only a powerful vision humans can use, individually and collectively, to design the world in which they live and act so that the possibility of flourishing is never closed off. (2008: 53–4)

Initiating and maintaining activity to avoid closure – from improving energy efficiency to eliminating use of fossil fuels – is extremely important because failure to do so creates the very real prospect that we will not be able to recover. Indeed, it is imperative to intensify substantially the amount of effort devoted to these activities to keep open the hope of universal flourishing.

This conception turns conventional understanding on its head. Ehrenfeld argues that much of our effort to enable sustainability is really about trying to drive *un*sustainability from our midst. Though it may sound like a word game, the point is critically serious: reducing unsustainability is not the same as moving toward sustainability. In other words, sustainability is not – and cannot be – merely about curtailing greenhouse-gas emissions, safeguarding biodiversity, reducing social inequality, and all the other important ambitions that get bundled into the contemporary sustainability discourse. As Ehrenfeld remarks: "without a vision, removing what is not sustainable will not work ... Sustainability is *not* the obverse of unsustainability ... [It] is a container for the highest set of human aspirations and associated cultural values" (2008: 54).

While intellectually robust, the task remains as to how to translate these metaphysical insights into workable actions. Ehrenfeld is keenly aware of this consideration and offers a few tentative recommendations. He observes that companies launch most consumer products into the world with scripts that implicitly and explicitly encourage consumerist lifestyles. Expressed in shorthand, the message is: "Buy me in the store[,] put me on at home[,] and then you're going to be beautiful" (Ehrenfeld 2009). Rather than convey this kind of aspiration, firms could design their offerings with different invocations that encouraged, for instance, ethical responsibility. Ehrenfeld likens this form of communication to speed bumps (he calls them "behavior-steering artifacts") that are purposefully placed to signal the need to slow down and drive with greater care.

Global citizens movement

Encouraged more by an intent to catalyze popular mobilization than to reformulate foundational principles is the work of the Great Transition Initiative (GTI) led by Paul Raskin of the Tellus Institute, a policy-oriented think-tank based in the United States.[7] This work evolved out of a prior project carried out by Raskin and his colleagues to formulate a series of prospective developmental pathways backcasted from the middle decades of the twenty-first century (Raskin et al. 2002; see also Raskin 2016) (see Box 4.3).

Raskin (2011) poses the question "How to change the world?" He and others associated with the GTI contend, consistent with the discussion earlier in this chapter, that global institutions are too feckless to drive the required transformations and businesses lack both the wherewithal and the aptitude to overcome their own narrowly construed commercial objectives. It is therefore necessary to "imagine the awakening of a new social actor: A coordinated global citizens movement (GCM) struggling on all fronts toward a just and sustainable planetary civilization" (2011: 4). This movement will need to overcome the often-debilitating fractures and fragmentation that currently exist within global civil society. Expanding on the popular movements that gave rise to nation states (and national identities) over the past few centuries, a GCM would enable a new form of consciousness and association stimulated by "[a] worldwide cultural and political awakening united under the banner Earth" (2011: 4). Initial expressions of this mobilization may have already begun to coalesce in the form of the World Social Forum, popular protests against various military campaigns, and climate-change strikes.

The incontrovertible task is to overcome the perpetuation of cause-oriented agendas and the lack of unifying organizational structures to harness this outpouring of civic craving to supersede existing institutions that are increasingly sclerotic and obsolescent. Raskin contends that "partial and dispersed actions, while laudatory, are insufficient in aggregate to open a new pathway for the global future. In the absence of an overarching vision and strategy, systemic deterioration on a larger scale overwhelms painstaking gains in specific locales and on particular issues" (2011: 4–5). To overcome current limitations, it will be necessary to conceive a new supranational identity along with the institutions to enable this insipient cognizance. This will need to be a polycentric undertaking modeled after the civil rights and labor movements in the United States.

> [A vitalized GCM] would promote a culture of peace and non-violence, nurturing ascendant values of human solidarity, ecological resilience, and quality of life. With adherents united by a shared identity as citizens of a nascent global culture and polity, a GCM would embrace diverse perspectives and movements in separate expressions of a common project. (2011: 5)

To activate this initiative, Raskin describes establishment of what he calls a "widening circle" mode of organization that pulls together the constituent elements into a vast network. This configuration will avoid "the specificity of place-based and issue based efforts [while connecting] people and groups working on a spectrum from local to global in a process of co-creation, always seeking to balance the equally valid principles of pluralism and unity" (2011: 5). Framed in such terms, transition to a so-called planetary phase of civilization will be dependent on several codependent shifts involving existential ways of knowing, cultural values, political institutions, human relations, and economic organization, but the argument is that popular mobilizations of engaged citizens will catalyze the envisaged process of systemic transformation.

Models for the next system

Triggered especially by the 2008 financial crisis, considerable interest has emerged in new heterodox thinking termed the "new economics" (see, for example, Speth 2008; Simms 2009; Jackson 2017; Schor 2010; Korten 2010). Central to the development of these perspectives has been the London-based New Economics Foundation (NEF) and the more recent work of The Next System Project (TNSP), launched in 2015 by historian and political economist Gar Alperovitz and environmental movement leader and author James (Gus) Speth.[8] Due to the breadth of this paradigm, the following discussion provides a condensed summary of the activities of the TNSP and encourages readers to seek out the cited sources for more details.

The TNSP is devoted to exploding the widely held myth that "there is no alternative" to the current dominant system of social and economic organization. This illusion is advanced in a variety of forums – political discussions, media reports, and debates at the bar – and claims that the current societal arrangement is the best we can do. Dysfunctional though it is, adherents of the status quo caution that other options would be far worse. They assert that we should be especially wary of overly ambitious and far-reaching proposals that call for "system change." Such ideas, it is claimed, are actually Trojan horses designed to undermine, and eventually abolish, capitalism.

The TNSP and others aligned with these perspectives respond that resistance to efforts to create the next system are both misinformed and wrong. We make a grave mistake when we presume that overexploitation of natural resources, environmental pollution, climate change, social inequality, racial injustice, and other contemporary crises are independent problems that can be adequately addressed on a selective basis. In truth, these challenges are different symptoms of a common and pervasive infirmity and we can only restore well-being by developing new visions, models, and pathways. As expressed on the TNSP website, the "next system [will be] radically different in fundamental ways from the failed systems of the past and present and capable of delivering superior social, economic, and ecological outcomes."[9]

The underlying conceptual framework for the next system is a "pluralist commonwealth" based on democratic ownership, decentralization, and community (Alperovitz 2016). This model of social and economic organization would reverse the massive accumulation of wealth by a small minority of people and rectify the shame of increasing income inequality that, over the past several decades, has become an incontrovertible feature of the United States and many other countries.

Further notable consequences of the prevailing system are massive consumer debt, deterioration of urban and rural communities, climate change, and endless war. According to Alperovitz, by more fairly distributing ownership of societal assets, we can transpose these processes and create opportunities for sustainability, democracy, and peace. He identifies several ways to achieve this objective.

First, cooperatives owned and operated by workers are at the heart of the overall conception because they emphasize community needs rather that maximization of profits that are then distributed to otherwise unaffiliated and remote shareholders. This organizational form also instills practical skills that encourage and enable democratic participation. As discussed in Chapter 5, better still is the establishment of institutional arrangements by municipal governments and others to configure cooperatives (and other nonprofit institutions and businesses) into larger confederated associations.

Second, participatory budgeting empowers citizens with a direct voice in prioritizing public expenditures. This institutional reform entails earmarking a portion of a government budget and creating mechanisms for residents to join in debates about how to allocate the funds. Implemented initially at the local level, this fiscal procedure gives people an opportunity to hone their citizenship skills and to develop understanding of the critical tradeoffs that are oftentimes part of allocative decision-making.

Finally, a pluralist commonwealth entails formation of alternative investment vehicles, including nonprofit credit unions, community-development organizations, and public banks to channel financial resources to projects and programs that make meaningful contributions to the social and economic vitality of their communities. Over time, this new societal infrastructure will provide viable options to mainstream banking, enhance local capabilities, and reduce the need for expensive public bailouts due to excessive risk-taking behavior and ineffectual regulatory oversight.

It is important to recognize that a pluralist commonwealth is just one vision of "the next system."[10] Other possibilities that contributors to the TNSP have advanced are predicated on commons-based peer production, solidarity economies organized around mutualism and pluralism, commitments to relocalization (or "neolocalization"), structures for economic governance that prioritize public ownership of critical societal assets, and degrowth (or postgrowth) economics. It is not always readily apparent how these ideas might fit together into a coherent paradigm or provide the basis for a workable political strategy, but we should not regard these challenges as limiting factors at this stage. The aim is to push out into discussion a wide range of proposals and to encourage their interaction and diffusion.

Conclusion

The concepts outlined in this chapter constitute a call to move beyond currently dominant understandings of sustainability. Advocates for these initiatives are motivated by recognition that, while efforts to implement new technologies and to achieve efficiency improvements have a role to play in systemic transformation, a successful transition is more likely to be impelled by social innovation predicated on new cultural values. It may not always be possible to articulate a well-delineated blueprint of what post-sustainability entails, but this is because the future will be collaboratively created in accordance with the resourcefulness that resides in specific places. We should not anticipate definitive "solutions" that governments can deploy on a top-down basis. Some readers may be altogether displeased by this approach and interpret it as a concession of defeat. Others with benevolent dispositions might nonetheless point to the high degree of uncertainty associated with the assorted proposals, the lack of preparedness for prospective introduction, and the likelihood of pernicious outcomes. These apprehensions are valid, but they need to be juxtaposed with current sustainability strategies that are unambiguously demonstrating rapidly diminishing returns.

Assembly of the six concepts presented here – and let us remember that this is just a selective representation of available alternatives – provides an opportunity to formulate a few general observations.

First, the era of post-sustainability is likely to be characterized by reduced emphasis on measurement and metrics. This will be disconcerting to sustainability scientists and practitioners accustomed to setting a course toward a predetermined target, but evolving understanding needs to be based on aligning processes of change with explicit moral principles rather than with data stored in a spreadsheet. The corollary of this observation is that it will be necessary to relinquish our fixation on control of how the future unfolds. Norgaard (1995: 487) effectively captures this situation:

> It is difficult if not impossible to predict what proves relatively more fit in the other subsystems as they coevolve with the whole system in which the initial change was introduced. And the process may go on, back and forth between the subsystems, in a positive feedback loop which may never equilibrate, making predication nearly impossible ... Maintaining diversity to keep options open, monitoring the changes, and adapting in order to "go with the flow" are the best we can do.

Second, in recent years sustainability has been largely subsumed by efforts to draw attention to the devastating impacts of climate change. This development is understandable given the consequences that will follow from rising greenhouse-gas emissions, especially for the least responsible and most vulnerable populations. As important as this challenge undeniably is, it would be a tragic mistake to regard our dependence on fossil fuels as a distinct problem rather than but one symptom of a much larger and systemic dilemma. It helps to remind ourselves of the famed statement attributed to army general and former president of the United States, Dwight Eisenhower, who said, "Whenever I run into a problem I can't solve, I always make it bigger. I can never solve it by trying to make it smaller, but if I make it big enough, I can begin to see the outlines of a solution." The insight is that ongoing efforts to ameliorate the climate crisis should be devoted to expanding rather than shrinking the scope of the undertaking.

Third, complicated and counterintuitive though it may be, we will need to become more comfortable with the concept of emergence. As Ehrenfeld (2009) explains, "[e]mergent properties cannot be fully explained by the workings of the parts ... In very simple terms, emergence is what we mean when we say the whole is greater than the sum of the parts. The emergent properties are usually what make complex systems interesting." Operationalizing this interpretation may ultimately prove to be less arduous than it initially seems. Most ordinary people are instinctively familiar with the idea from encounters with elusive phenomena like beauty and love. Reforming the disposition of scientists, engineers, and policymakers who have been acculturated to pay little heed to these considerations is apt to be a more difficult task.

Finally, we desperately need new conceptions of how to reconcile the global and the local. Despite the appeals of environmentalists during the 1970s to "think globally and act locally," understanding of globalization over the past several decades has disproportionately privileged international trade. A concomitant process of commodification has led to the homogenization of cultures and the withering of local capacity in an excessively large number of communities. Raskin seeks to recapture the intent of the earlier mantra: "Rather than a global monoculture that overrides the specificity of place-based and issue-based efforts, the aim would be to connect people and groups working on a spectrum from local to global in a process of co-creation, always seeking to balance the equally valid principles of pluralism and unity" (2011: 5).

It is, of course, not difficult to feel demoralized and to conclude that the challenges are too overwhelming. However, if we take a careful look around, we are likely to observe indications of transformation. This evidence may be small and fragile, but if we open our eyes wide enough, the evidence is impossible to miss. It may take the form of a community garden, a maker space, a cooperative grocery store, or a group of friends plotting a new venture in a downtown coffee shop. Many of these pursuits will fail, but eventually more will thrive, though it will be hard to discern in advance how it will all play out. One thing we do know is that national and international institutions of governance, despite nearly unimaginable resources, have repeatedly and tragically demonstrated their complicity in the existing system and cannot serve as reliable stewards of sustainability (or whatever we might call its successor). The future will be created by the germination and propagation of multitudes of local initiatives. This process is apt to be hopelessly chaotic and indeterminate, but push through we must. After all, what choice do we have?

Afterword: Sustainability in the Era of COVID-19

I approach the writing of this afterword with a large measure of trepidation. A first draft of the manuscript for this book was completed just as the COVID-19 pandemic was claiming its first victims in China at the start of January 2020 and others in Asia were beginning to come to grips with the lethality of the crisis. I was working on the revisions two months later when Italy and Spain both came under lockdown and the United States declared a national emergency. It is now the beginning of April, and the calamity continues its rampage throughout Europe, North America, and other parts of the world. And the epidemiological models indicate that it is still early days. Prevailing estimates are that the coronavirus pandemic will take the lives of more than 100,000 people in the United States and multifold times this number globally. We are indeed living through the season of the plague.

But this is just the aggregate human toll. The coronavirus outbreak is simultaneously a public health emergency and a source of profound social and economic disruption. There is little reason to suspect that in the coming months the scale of misfortune will become smaller rather than larger. It is frightening to anticipate what may unfold in the months-long period between the writing of these words and when readers will have the opportunity to cast their eyes across the printed page on which they appear.

A dozen years ago, the ecological economist Peter Victor published a notable volume of his own entitled *Managing Without Growth: Slower by Design, Not Disaster.* As it turns out, the alliterative mantra in the subtitle was prescient. Through mostly polite entreaties, sustainability scientists and activists have sought over the past few decades to encourage humanity to take better account of its relationship with the biosphere. As we have seen in the preceding chapters, the appeals took the form of staging international megaconferences, offering proposals for new systems of governance, innovating cutting-edge technologies, and calling for less resource-intensive lifestyles. These propositions, we unfortunately need to acknowledge, have had marginal effect and we now find ourselves confronting the second part of Victor's binary.

The prospect of disaster as an occasion for serious appraisal has been primarily understood as emanating from the threats of climate change. However, as a practical matter, societal engagement on this issue was always going to be an uphill struggle because of its lack of immediacy – at least in most places. In a world in which there is no shortage of problems, it has been much easier to kick the can down the road or, at least for some people, to mischaracterize the risks posed by excessive greenhouse-gas emissions as simply the angry rage of anticapitalists and other malcontents. We now find ourselves very much caught up in a different kind of disaster, one that does not creep forward in small increments of temperature or sea level, but instead through a rapidly spreading contagion that ravages human bodies, economies, and healthcare systems.

As a partial corrective for the fact that preparation of this book was not specifically informed by the onset of COVID-19, the editors at Polity have generously given me the opportunity to include this afterword. My aim is to consider the impact of the coronavirus outbreak on several of the themes discussed in earlier chapters and to offer a few speculative observations on the implications of the crisis from the vantage point of sustainability.

For society writ large, COVID-19 – and for that matter any significant adverse event – is roughly analogous to a stress test that an individual with predisposing medical concerns might be advised to undergo as part of a precautionary evaluation. Such an examination would deliver a status report on general healthfulness and identify any latent conditions that might justify preemptive intervention. In a similar sense, major disasters compel affected countries and their constituent communities to demonstrate their capacity for resilience and to disclose underlying features that under customary circumstances are hidden from widespread view. With a few national exceptions, the accumulated evidence to date has not imparted an affirming appraisal of our well-being. It is reasonable to presuppose that had the supplications of sustainability scientists been taken more seriously in prior decades, the tragedy of the pandemic might not have been so grave. The following discussion considers three issues that the present crisis has unambiguously exposed.

First, the contagion has made painfully clear that the pre-COVID-19 global economy was built on an extremely fragile foundation. Reduction in consumer demand and elimination of a few days of revenue for businesses prompted most of the system to promptly crumble. In the United States, more than 20 million people submitted claims for unemployment insurance during the two months following the emergency declaration and the number will regrettably rise in coming months. In Denmark, Germany, and several other rich countries, finance ministries have pledged to cover a significant share of the wage bill, but it remains to be seen how long they can maintain their commitments before buckling under the weight of the fiscal burden. Legislatures and parliaments have rushed through "stimulus plans" that are, at least at this stage, better understood as "survival payments" to protect many households and companies from complete and probably unrecoverable collapse. More is sure to follow. Stalwart advocates of austerity who disingenuously contended that there was simply no money to address social needs have posthaste become ardent champions of prodigious public assistance.

Second, the coronavirus outbreak has made it impossible to ignore any longer the contribution of the "care economy" to societal prosperity. Most policymakers have purposefully ignored the role that childcare, eldercare, volunteer work, and other unpaid forms of labor play in enabling the functioning of the "real economy." It seems, at least from the perspective of the moment, that it will be politically irresponsible to maintain this delusion. GDP and other similar metrics discussed in Chapter 2 have likely lost their bewitching lure, and will – we can hope – be supplanted by more robust and meaningful alternatives. This process of replacement is likely to be accelerated over the foreseeable future because conventional measures of societal welfare based on material and energy throughput will not confer reassuring feedback.

Finally, COVID-19 has highlighted in unequivocal terms the perverse levels of inequality and social inequity that have been allowed to take hold in most rich countries. Perhaps as much as a third of the population in these nations have the privilege during periods of quarantine to retreat from customary workplaces and to earn a livelihood from the relative safety of their homes using online tools. The majority of people have either been quickly rendered unemployed or required to labor under dangerous circumstances where they put their health at risk on a daily basis. I am also afraid that in due course a comprehensive accounting of impacts will reveal that the effects on mental health, especially as evinced by domestic violence, will be profound. The ramifications of the contagion on poorer countries with weak and already overstretched medical systems is hard to fathom at present, but will be indescribably severe.

It is difficult to underestimate the scale of current suffering or to assess the challenges that are ahead. Nonetheless, for readers interested in the prospect of an environmentally tenable and socially equitable future, extant circumstances are a moment of reckoning. As outlined in Chapter 4 when discussing the Multi-Level Perspective, we are in the midst of a rare and massive shift in landscape conditions. Proposals for social reform that were at one time dismissed as unrealistic or infeasible are being implemented at breakneck speed. For instance, governments are creating programs to deliver what is, effectively speaking, a universal basic income. It is additionally plausible to expect that, by the time this book is available, calls for moratoriums on rent and mortgage payments will have been enacted in the most adversely affected areas.

Policymakers are taking other actions with potentially far-reaching ramifications. In the realm of urban mobility, mayors are banning vehicular traffic from major thoroughfares and repurposing the roadways as recreational corridors at the same time that they are eliminating fares for public transportation. Perhaps most significantly, governments are nationalizing key industries with early notable cases including the takeover of Alitalia by the Italian state and a similar move in the United Kingdom to rescue the national railway system. These initiatives are being rushed forward out of a sense of economic urgency rather than a commitment to sustainability, but they will be difficult to reverse and could, over time, prove to be an important factor in enabling the kinds of transitions that have been heralded in this book.

In short, what was previously deemed impossible has suddenly become achievable. While it is hard to know the ultimate extent of these developments, some unique and interesting possibilities can be envisaged. We obviously need to maintain measured expectations, but calls to "return to normal" may prove to be little more than the plaintive and revanchist pleas of elites who see their privileges – and the political and financial rewards that have flowed from them – slipping away.

Of course, there is no assurance that a turn to sustainability will occur during the aftermath of COVID-19. The future will be contingent on a multitude of decisions and certainly not all of them will be premised on hopefulness and solidarity. Even at the current juncture, there are indications that some countries are using the pandemic to institute more restrictive border controls, to roll back environmental protections, to inflame xenophobia, and to reinforce autocratic power. Aside from these cynical moves, accurately forecasting the impacts of both specific initiatives and wider social changes is conceptually complicated because of the perils of correctly ascertaining intricate feedback loops and indirect causal chains.

The market for fossil fuels provides a salient example. The initial spread of contagion prompted a precipitous drop in oil demand, depressing global prices which, at the time of this writing, were a shade above $20 per barrel. Many smaller-scale producers, unless able to secure a public bailout, will become insolvent. Such a wave of bankruptcies might initially seem like a propitious development, but over the longer term will enhance the market control of major players like Saudi Arabia and Russia. In addition, persistently low prices will undermine financial justification for solar and wind investments and hence stall progress toward a renewables transition, as well as displacement of gasoline-powered automobiles. By contrast, as fossil fuels become less profitable, we could see the reallocation of financial capital to other energy sectors that promise more lucrative returns. These conflicting tendencies make forecasting the eventual outcome a tricky undertaking.

Changes in consumer behavior – curtailment of air travel, reduction of work-related commuting, decrease in purchases of discretionary products, increase in cooking at home, expanded use of videoconferencing for both professional and personal purposes – raise similar conundrums. It is unquestionably true that resource throughput has been declining as households have hunkered down and adapted themselves to slower lifestyles. The imposition of social distancing has combined with a cold shutdown of many businesses and led to economic contraction of a previously unimaginable magnitude. We are furthermore witnessing the emergence of new conceptions of how to renegotiate the balance between work and nonwork aspects of our lives.

It is difficult to anticipate which new practices will be maintained over the longer term and which will revert to earlier form. Much will presumably depend on the length of the public health emergency. It is, though, useful to note that no responsible advocate of sustainable consumption or economic degrowth would consider the current disaster-impelled approach an advisable way to adjust the scale of human activities to planetary boundaries. What is true is that lockdown-induced retrenchment has enabled people to experience what life would be like, roughly speaking, if we were really serious about the notion of one-planet living or intent on holding the rise in average global temperature to the 1.5°C threshold that climate scientists urge as necessary to prevent catastrophic harm.

For the moment, it is premature to pass judgment about the prospects of the ambitious sustainability-informed programs that have been politically reactivated in the wake of COVID-19 and advanced as off-the-shelf strategies to reinvigorate economic life. Drawing on ideas first proposed during the aftermath of the 2008 financial crisis, the European Union has expressed intent in pursuing a Green Deal or a Coronavirus "Marshall Plan." Present formulations combine roadmaps for economic growth – involving vast public investments in smart electrical grids, low-carbon technologies, and electric and autonomous vehicles – with calls for "future-proofing" companies by encouraging new business models based on net-zero emissions.

While the politics are more torturous and convoluted in the United States, similar policy proposals for a Green New Deal are being promoted as "green stimulus." Recommended strategies include retraining oil and gas industry workers to install equipment for carbon capture and storage, research in low-carbon aircraft, deployment of electric vehicles for use by the taxi industry, and new investments in renewable energy infrastructure. Assuming the package gains traction in coming months, the list of elements is likely to grow longer.

In conclusion, a repercussion of COVID-19 is that it has revealed our failure to steer civilization toward a more sustainable future. The coronavirus pandemic is not separate from climate change, biodiversity loss, income inequality, social marginalization, political disempowerment, and the full range of issues set forth by the United Nations SDGs. Our experience with the contagion holds numerous lessons that we can usefully apply to these related pending and portentous dilemmas. The most important insight may involve the negation of lies falsely asserting that social change is inconceivable and the costs are unbearable. We quite clearly have the capacity to adapt, and to do so with urgency and resolve.

Notes

Chapter 1 What Is Sustainability?

1 Notable as well were "people-to-people" volunteer-assistance programs such as the Peace Corps created in the United States and the Swedish International Development Authority (now Swedish International Development Cooperation Agency).

2 The community of NGOs active in providing various forms of development assistance includes Save the Children (established in 1919), Oxfam (established in 1942), and Catholic Relief Services (established in 1943).

3 Starting with the years immediately following World War II, McCormick (1986) usefully traces out the chronology of activities that led up to the *World Conservation Strategy*. Though the IUCN was the lead organization responsible for preparation of the report, it was developed in collaboration with UNEP, the Food and Agriculture Organization of the United Nations, UNESCO, and the World Wildlife Fund.

4 Economists Barbara Ward and Kenneth Boulding and ecological designer Buckminster Fuller separately popularized the concept of "Spaceship Earth," though there had been earlier uses of related ideas. Ecologist Garrett Hardin conceived and promoted the notion of a "lifeboat" (or "lifeboat ethics").

5 The ten countries with the highest fertility rates (in 2017) are predominantly located in sub-Saharan Africa and comprise Niger (6.49), Angola (6.16), Mali (6.01), Burundi (5.99), Somalia (5.80), Burkina Faso (5.71), Uganda (5.71), Zambia (5.63), Malawi (5.49), and Afghanistan (5.12).

6 See https://americanrhetoric.com/speeches/jimmycartercrisisofconfidence. htm for a video and transcript of the speech.

7 Brundtland was trained as a medical doctor and came to be highly

regarded for her background in the field of public health, having been the Norwegian Environment Minster for five years during the 1970s. She ultimately served three terms as Prime Minister (1981, 1986–89, and 1990–96).

8 Johnson et al. (2007) counted the appearance of more than 140 alternative definitions during the two years following publication of the Brundtland Report. They further estimated the existence at the time of approximately 300 definitions of "sustainable development" and "sustainability" just within the area of environmental management and allied disciplines.

9 See https://www.unenvironment.org/about-un-environment. This process of clarifying UNEP's role within the UN system was completed in December 2012 when the General Assembly resolved to "strengthen and upgrade" the organization, a process that has included establishing universal membership in its governing body and creating a source of more stable and secure funding.

10 See   https://sustainabledevelopment.un.org/post2015/transformingour world.

Chapter 2 The Science of Sustainability

1 Important precursors of MAB were the International Geophysical Year (1957–58) and the International Biological Program (1964–74). See Schleper (2017) for further details.

2 The term Anthropocene first gained wide exposure a couple of years later with an article by Nobel laureate Paul Crutzen (2002), published in the journal *Nature*. As noted by Hamilton and Grinevald (2015) and Lowenthal (2016), the concept actually dates back at least as far as the mid-nineteenth century, and expressions of the essential notion can be found in a broad array of foundational environmental ideas.

3 Stratigraphy is the study of the sequencing of strata or rock layers according to the geologic time scale. The Geological Society of London is the oldest professional association for the geological sciences; working in conjunction with the International Commission on Stratigraphy and the International Union of Geological Sciences, it serves as the official arbiter of issues of geological significance.

4 The more formal stratigraphical term is a Global Boundary Stratotype Section and Point (GSSP). An alternative (and less rigorous) approach, generally used for dating the oldest geological phenomena, is called the Global Standard Stratigraphic Age (GSSA) and involves setting a time boundary without the need for stratigraphic evidence. After extensive debate, the WGA decided to opt for the use of a GSSP to determine the start date of the Anthropocene.

5 Calculations are based on the 2016 edition of the National Footprint Accounts (using 2012 data).

Chapter 3 Engineering a More Sustainable Future

1 Though it is a minor quibble, Gore deploys the quotation somewhat out of context. Dubbed Dornbusch's Law, the original formulation is "Crises take longer to arrive than you can possibly imagine, but when they do come, they happen faster than you possibly imagine."

2 Quoted at https://scribepublications.com.au/explore/video-audio/the-conundrum. See also Owen (2011).

3 As outlined by Phipps (2018), it merits noting that, because of the tendency for clothing-rental platforms to lower the cost of access and to shorten fashion cycles for popular garments, any actual sustainability benefits of this business model are extremely questionable.

4 This latter proposition is likely to become increasingly relevant. For instance, the President of Indonesia recently announced plans to relocate the nation's capital to a newly built city on the island of Borneo. Motivating this ambitious project is recognition that Jakarta is sinking and unrecoverably polluted. These conditions are deemed to defy remediation in an era of climate change and ongoing seismic activity, so a purpose-built alternative is seen as offering a more promising answer.

5 There are many formulations of this observation, but the original presentation is generally attributed to Barry Commoner (1971). He asserted four laws of ecology, the first two of which are relevant in the current context: "everything is connected to everything else" and "everything must go somewhere." The other two laws are "nature knows best" and "there is no such thing as a free lunch."

6 A related social practice has been to redeploy an older refrigerator to the basement or garage rather than scrapping it when an upgrade is made to the primary kitchen-based unit. A household that previously operated a single refrigerator thus ends up running two appliances. By contrast, there is a subculture of individuals who in recent years have opted to live without a refrigerator as a novel form of frugal living (Kurutz 2009).

7 For treatment of the more technical dimensions of this discussion, see Polimeni et al. (2007) and Herring and Sorrell (2009).

8 Refer to Huesemann and Huesemann (2011) for a more comprehensive analysis. Also useful is a video lecture available at https://ratical.org/ratville/AoS/MHuesemann102514.html.

Chapter 4 Planning Sustainability Transitions

1 SDG 12 calls for "responsible consumption and production," while allocation of resources more generally is either explicit or implicit in most of the other goals.

2 Other widely used methodologies for assessing the future include the

Delphi technique, foresight analysis, time-series analysis, environmental scanning, and content analysis.

3 It is important not to discount the role that various intermediaries play in shaping the performance of urban sociotechnical systems. See Guy et al. (2012) for a comprehensive analysis of the NGOs, consultants, and other actors engaged in these activities.

4 The list of other cities with congestion-pricing schemes includes Singapore, Milan, and Gothenburg. New York City announced in 2019 plans to implement a fee-based system to enter Manhattan with a car and there is at the time of writing speculation that this development could trigger a wave of other municipal governments to take similar action.

5 A related strategy has been to encourage the adoption of "car-free days," which are scheduled in advance and designed to encourage people to conduct lifestyle experiments that do not involve reliance on an automobile. Some cities have also established temporary car-free zones as a way to create opportunities to experience parts of the urban environment in novel ways. An especially effective example of this strategy is Paris Plages, which involves closing down the roadway along the river Seine during the summer and creating artificial beaches.

6 Such cities have also been termed "wired cities," "cyber cities," "digital cities," "intelligent cities," and "sentient cities."

7 Martin et al. (2019) develop the concept of the "urban smart-sustainability fix" as part of their critique of the technological bias inherent in most formulations of the smart city.

8 The five surges (and their starting dates) outlined by TEP are the Industrial Revolution (1771), the Age of Steam and Railways (1829), the Age of Steel, Electricity, and Heavy Engineering (1875), the Age of Oil, the Automobile, and Mass Production (1908), and the Age of Information and Telecommunications (1971).

9 Schot and Kanger (2018) observe somewhat worryingly that if we rely on the timing of the prior five surges, Perez's anticipated green ICT revolution should have started during the early 2000s, but evidence of such a transition is clearly not yet apparent. We seem instead to be stalled in a protracted period of increasing social (and political) distress whereby the existing paradigm is evermore obsolete and arrival of its replacement is long overdue because of failure by policymakers to implement the necessary structural reforms and establish the required facilitating mechanisms. In the absence of these interventions, according to Perez, it may take several surges to break the impasse (or "blocked transition") caused by lingering neoliberal commitments.

10 It should be apparent that there is similarity between Schot and Kanger's notion of Deep Transitions and the concepts of the Anthropocene and the Great Acceleration discussed in Chapter 2.

11 It is at the same time necessary not to overemphasize the role of countries as the primary unit of analysis given the high level of interconnectivity across industries, civil society, scientific communities, and so forth. It may be the case that, rather than sustainability transitions taking

place across national sociotechnical systems, associated processes of innovation are apt to occur in particular subsectors or on a partial basis across different geographic scales.

Chapter 5 Social Innovation and Sustainability

1 This characterization does not mean to suggest that there were not during this period countermovements based on tacit or alternative forms of knowledge that challenged the authority of conventional experts. In recent years, it has been increasingly common to suggest that the pendulum has swung in the opposite direction and that there has been a "death of expertise" (Nicholas 2018).

2 Authorship of the article is attributed to the Forbes Technology Council, which describes itself as "an invitation-only community for world-class CIOs [chief information officers], CTOs [chief technology officers] and technology executives" and claims to be a "highly-selective, quality-over quantity organization." Members need to generate a minimum of $5 million of revenue or have a minimum of $5 million in financing.

3 Sociologist Fred Block (2008) advances a partially contrasting view that claims the United States has a "hidden developmental state."

4 Shared-use facilities are actually more commonplace than is conventionally thought to be the case; in terms of transportation and travel, the category includes conventional taxis, rental cars, ski lifts, hotels, trains, airplanes, and so forth. With respect to the case of second-hand apparel, sharing can take a number of different forms – borrowing, bartering, cooperative purchasing, swapping, donating, consigning, pawning, repurposing, gifting, and bequeathing.

5 For information on the Sharing Cities Alliance, see https://sharingcitiesalliance.com. Details about the Sharing Cities Program is at http://www.sharingcities.eu and for the Sharing Cities Network at https://www.shareable.net/sharing-cities-network.

6 See https://www.ifixit.com.

7 As detailed in Yourgrau (2015), an understanding of Marie Kondō as a marketing phenomenon requires recognizing that a large Japanese publisher of self-help books has played a significant role in creating her celebrity persona. In addition, her website now features an online store that sells highly stylized home décor.

8 See https://www.aei.org/carpe-diem/new-us-homes-today-are-1000-square-feet-larger-than-in-1973-and-living-space-per-person-has-nearly-doubled.

9 See http://scitech.blogs.cnn.com/2008/08/13/the-pacific-toilet-bowl-that-never-flushes/.

Chapter 6 Toward Post-Sustainability?

1 See https://climateactiontracker.org/about/.

2 Most sustainability scientists will justifiably regard the characterization advanced by Benson and Craig as a managerialist caricature based on an interpretation of stationarity that has little resemblance to how leading proponents have articulated the foundations of a steady-state economy. For instance, a steady-state economy is not generally envisioned as a static system but, rather, is about maintaining a constant stock of physical capital and under such conditions can still be highly dynamic and innovative.

3 Some authors make a distinction between regenerative development, regenerative design, and regenerative sustainability (see Mang and Reed 2012; Cole 2012b; and Robinson and Cole 2015).

4 See http://www.oberlinproject.org/.

5 Deep Ecology originates in the work of Norwegian environmental philosopher Arne Næss (see, for example, Drengson and Devall 2010).

6 Sen's work on the Capabilities Approach was carried out partly in collaboration with the philosopher Martha Nussbaum, who has made her own contributions to its current formulation. This framework, as discussed in Chapter 2, provides the foundation for design of the HDI. The notion of capabilities informed design of both the MDGs and the SDGs. Furthermore, Sen was Economic Advisor for the Commission on the Measurement of Economic Performance and Social Progress (commonly referred to as the Stiglitz-Sen-Fitoussi Commission), convened by the French government in 2008.

7 See https://greattransition.org/.

8 For details on the New Economics Foundation, see https://neweconomics. org. Information on the Next System Project is at https://thenextsystem.org.

9 See https://thenextsystem.org/about-next-system-project.

10 See https://thenextsystem.org/learn/collections/new-systems-possibilities-and-proposals.

References

Acemoglu, Daron, and James Robinson. 2019. *The Narrow Corridor: States, Societies, and the Fate of Liberty*. New York: Penguin Press.

Adler, David. 2019. Kulturindustrie and the Green New Deal. *IPPR Progressive Review* 26(2): 188–195.

Agyeman, Julian, and Bob Evans. 2004. "Just sustainability": The emerging discourse of environmental justice in Britain? *Geographical Journal* 170(2): 155–164.

Alcarez, Olga, Pablo Buenestado, Beatriz Escribano, Barbara Sureda, Albert Turon, and Josep Xercavins. 2018. Distributing the global carbon budget with climate justice criteria. *Climatic Change* 149(2): 131–145.

Almlund, Pernille, Per Homann Jespersen, and Søren Riis, eds. 2012. *Rethinking Climate Change Research: Clean Technology, Culture, and Communication*. New York: Routledge.

Alperovitz, Gar. 2016. The pluralist commonwealth. *The Next System Project*, September 3.

Anderson, Chris. 2012. *Makers: The New Industrial Revolution*. New York: Crown.

Antal, Miklów, and Jeroen van den Bergh. 2013. Macroeconomics, financial crisis, and the environment: Strategies for a sustainability transition. *Environmental Innovation and Societal Transitions* 6: 47–66.

Applebaum, Binyamin. 2019. *The Economists' Hour: False Prophets, Free Markets, and the Fracture of Society*. New York: Little, Brown and Company.

Arcadis. 2016. *Sustainable Cities Index 2016*. Amsterdam: Arcadis.

Asatu-Adjaye, John, Linus Blomqvist, Stewart Brand, Barry Brook, Ruth DeFries, ... and Peter Teague. 2016. *An Ecomodernist Manifesto*. Oakland, CA: Breakthrough Institute.

Barbier, Edward. 2010. *A Global Green New Deal: Rethinking the Economic Recovery*. New York: Cambridge University Press.

Benson, Melinda, and Robin Craig. 2014. The end of sustainability. *Society and Natural Resources* 27: 777–782.

Benyus, Janine. 1997. *Biomimicry: Innovation Inspired by Nature*. New York: William Morrow.

Berry, Wendell. 1993. *Sex, Economy, Freedom and Community: Eight Essays*. New York: Pantheon.

Block, Fred. 2008. Swimming against the current: The rise of a hidden developmental state in the United States. *Politics and Society* 36(2): 169–206.

Boeckmann, Margaret. 1976. Policy impacts of the New Jersey income maintenance experiment. *Policy Sciences* 7(1): 53–76.

Böhringer, Christoph, and Patrick Jochem. 2007. Measuring the immeasurable: a survey of sustainability indices. *Ecological Economics* 63: 1–8.

Bok, Derek. 2010. *The Politics of Happiness: What Government Can Learn from the New Research on Well-Being*. Princeton, NJ: Princeton University Press.

Borowy, Iris. 2014. *Defining Sustainable Development for Our Common Future. A History of the World Commission on Environment and Development (Brundtland Commission)*. New York: Routledge.

Boström, Magnus. 2012. A missing pillar? Challenges in theorizing and practicing social sustainability: introduction to the special issue. *Sustainability: Science, Practice, and Policy* 8(1): 3–14.

Bostrom, Nick. 2016. *Superintelligence: Paths, Dangers, Strategies*. New York: Oxford University Press.

Botsman, Rachel, and Roo Rogers. 2010. *What's Mine Is Yours: The Rise of Collaborative Consumption*. New York: Harper Business.

Boulding, Kenneth. 1966. The economics of the coming spaceship Earth, pp. 3–14 in Henry Jarrett, ed., *Environmental Quality in a Growing Economy*. Baltimore, MD: Johns Hopkins University Press.

Brandt Commission. 1983. *Common Crisis North–South: Cooperation for World Recovery*. Cambridge, MA: MIT Press.

Bringezu, Stefan. 2009. Visions of a sustainable resource use, pp. 155–215 in Stefan Bringezu and Raimund Bleischwitz, eds., *Sustainable Resource Management: Global Trends, Visions, and Policies*. Sheffield: Greenleaf.

Brown, J. Christopher, and Mark Purcell. 2005. There's nothing inherent about scale: Political ecology, the local trap, and the politics of development in the Brazilian Amazon, *Geoforum* 36: 607–624.

Brunneder, Johanna, and Utpal Dholakia. 2018. The self-creation effect: making a product supports its mindful consumption and the consumer's well-being. *Market Letters* 29: 377–389.

Brynfolfsson, Erik, and Andrew McAfee. 2014. *The Second Machine Age: Work, Progress and Prosperity in a Time of Brilliant Technologies*. New York: W. W. Norton.

Calnitsky, David. 2016. "More normal than welfare": The Mincome experiment, stigma, and community experience. *Canadian Review of Sociology* 53(1): 26–71.

Capra, Fritjof. 1984. *The Turning Point: Science, Society, and the Rising Culture*. New York: Bantam.

Cellina, Francesa, Roberta Castri, José Veiga Simão, and Pasquale Granato. 2020. Co-creating app-based policy measures for mobility behavior change: A trigger for novel governance practices at the urban level. *Sustainable Cities and Society* 53. https://doi.org/10.1016/j.scs.2019.101911.

Chinchilla, Izaskun, and Emilio Luque. 2019. Which beauty will guide us? Seeking a reflective, sustainable, socially engaged visual culture. *Architectural Design* 89(5): 46–51.

Christofferson, Bill. 2004. *The Man from Clear Lake: Earth Day Founder Senator Gaylord Nelson*. Madison, WI: University of Wisconsin Press.

Cohen, Maurie. 2017. *The Future of Consumer Society: Prospects for Sustainability in the New Economy*. New York: Oxford University Press.

Cohen, Maurie. 2020. New conceptions of sufficient home size in high-income countries: Are we approaching a sustainable consumption transition? *Housing, Theory and Society*, February 3. https://doi.org/10.1 080/14036096.2020.1722218.

Cole, Raymond. 2012a. Regenerative design and development: Current theory and practice. *Building Research and Information* 40(1): 1–6.

Cole, Raymond. 2012b. Transitioning from green to regenerative design. *Building Research and Information* 40(1): 39–53.

Commoner, Barry. 1971. *The Closing Circle: Nature, Man, and Technology*. New York: Random House.

Cosgrove, Denis. 1994. Contested global visions: *One-World, Whole-Earth*, and the Apollo space photographs. *Annals of the Association of American Geographers* 84(2): 270–294.

Cox, Stan. 2010. *Losing Our Cool: Uncomfortable Truths About Our Air-Conditioned World (and Finding New Ways to Get Through Summer)*. New York: New Press.

Crowley, Kate, and Brian Head. 2017. The enduring challenge of "wicked problems": Revising Rittel and Webber. *Policy Sciences* 50(4): 539–547.

Crutzen, Paul. 2002. Geology of mankind. *Nature* 415(6687): 23.

Crutzen, Paul, and Eugene Stoermer. 2000. The Anthropocene. *Global Change Newsletter* 41: 17–18.

Daneshvar, Fariborz, Pouyan Negadhashemi, Zhen Zhang, and Matthew Herman. 2018. Assessing the relative importance of parameter estimation in stream health based environmental justice modeling. *Journal of Hydrology* 563: 211–222.

Davies, Anna. 2014. Co-creating sustainable eating futures: Technology, ICT, and citizen-consumer ambivalence. *Futures* 62: 181–193.

Davies, Jeremy. 2018. *The Birth of the Anthropocene*. Berkeley: University of California Press.

De Haan, Fjalar, Briony Ferguson, Rachelle Adamowicz, Phillip Johnstone, Rebekah Brown, and Tony Wong. 2014. The needs of society: A new understanding of transitions, sustainability, and livability. *Technological Forecasting and Social Change* 85: 121–132.

Dhiman, Satinder, and Joan Marques. 2016. *Spirituality and Sustainability: New Horizons and Exemplary Approaches*. New York: Springer.

Drengson, Alan, and Bill Devall. 2010. *The Ecology of Wisdom: Writings of Arne Næss*. Berkeley, CA: Counterpoint.

Dryzek, John. 2019. *The Politics of the Anthropocene*. New York: Oxford University Press.

du Plessis, Chrisna. 2012. Towards a regenerative paradigm for the built environment. *Building Research and Information* 40(1): 7–22.

Dutton, Andrea, Anders Carlson, Antony Long, Glenn Milne, Peter Clark, … Maureen Raymo. 2015. Sea-level rise due to polar ice-sheet mass loss during past warm periods. *Science* 349(6244): 153–162.

Eames, Malcolm, Tim Dixon, Tim May, and Miriam Hunt. 2013. City futures: Exploring urban retrofit and sustainable transitions. *Building Research and Information* 41(5): 504–516.

Eckersley, Robin. 2006. Progress, sustainability and human well-being: Is a new worldview emerging? *Journal of Innovation and Sustainable Development* 1(4): 304–317.

Ehrenfeld, John. 2008. *Sustainability by Design: A Subversive Strategy for Transforming Our Consumer Culture*. New Haven, CT: Yale University Press.

Ehrenfeld, John. 2009. Flourishing forever. *MIT Sloan Management Review*, July 14. https://sloanreview.mit.edu/article/flourishing-forever/.

Ellis, Erle. 2018. Science alone won't save the Earth. People have to do that. *New York Times*, August 11.

Elzen, Boelie, Frank Geels, and Ken Green, eds. 2004. *System Innovation and the Transition to Sustainability: Theory, Evidence, and Policy*. Northampton, MA: Edward Elgar.

Ericson, Torgeir, Björn Kjønstad, and Anders Barstad. 2014. Mindfulness and sustainability. *Ecological Economics* 104: 73–79.

Feldman, Corinna, and Ulrich Hamm. 2015. Consumers' perceptions and preferences for local food: a review. *Food Quality and Preference* 40 (Part A): 152–164.

Forbes Technology Council. 2017. Solving social problems: 11 ways new tech can help. *Forbes*, 2 October.

Foster, John. 2014. *After Sustainability: Denial, Hope, Retrieval*. London: Earthscan.

Foster, John. 2017a. Hope after sustainability: Tragedy and transformation. *Global Discourse* 7: 1–9.

Foster, John, ed. 2017b. *Post-Sustainability: Tragedy and Transformation*. New York: Routledge.

Friedman, Thomas. 2007. The power of green. *New York Times*, April 15.

Fuller, Buckminster. 1970. *Operating Manual for Spaceship Earth*. Carbondale, IL: Southern Illinois University Press.

Furman, Jeffrey, Michael Porter, and Scott Stern. 2002. The determinants of national innovative capacity. *Research Policy* 31(6): 899–933.

Gansky, Lisa. 2010. *The Mesh: Why the Future of Business Is Sharing*. New York: Portfolio/Penguin.

Geels, Frank. 2002. Technological transitions as evolutionary reconfiguration processes: A multi-level perspective and a case study. *Research Policy* 31(8–9): 1257–1274.

Geels, Frank. 2005. *Technological Transitions and System Innovations: A Co-Evolutionary and Socio-Technical Analysis.* Northampton, MA: Edward Elgar.

Geels, Frank. 2013. The impact of the financial economic crisis on sustainability transitions: Financial investment governance and public discourse. *Environmental Innovation and Societal Transitions* 65: 67–95.

Gershenfeld, Neil. 2005. *Fab: The Coming Revolution on Your Desktop: From Personal Computers to Personal Fabrication.* New York: Basic Books.

Glotfelty, Cheryll, and Eve Quesnel. 2014. *The Biosphere and the Bioregion: Essential Writings of Peter Berg.* New York: Routledge.

Gore, Al. 2019. It's not too late. *New York Times*, September 22.

Gottlieb, Robert. 1993. *Forcing the Spring: The Transformation of the American Environmental Movement.* Washington, DC: Island Press.

Green New Deal Group. 2008. *A Green New Deal.* London: New Economics Foundation.

Guthman, Julie. 2008. Neoliberalism and the making of food politics in California. *Geoforum* 29(3): 1171–1183.

Guy, Simon, Simon Marvin, Will Medd, and Timothy Moss. 2012. *Shaping Urban Infrastructures and the Governance of Socio-technical Networks.* London: Routledge.

Haddad, Lawrence, Endang Achadi, Mohamed Bendech, Arti Ahuja, Komal Bhatia, ... K. Srinath Reddy. 2015. The Global Nutrition Report 2014: Actions and accountability to accelerate the world's progress on nutrition. *Journal of Nutrition* 145(4): 663–671.

Hajer, Maarten. 1995. *The Politics of Environmental Discourse: Ecological Modernization and the Policy Process.* New York: Oxford University Press.

Halliday, Stephen. 2001. *The Great Stink of London: Sir Joseph Bazalgette and the Cleansing of the Victorian Metropolis.* Stroud, Gloucestershire: Sutton.

Hamilton, Clive, and Jacques Grinevald. 2015. Was the Anthropocene anticipated? *Anthropocene Review* 3(1): 52–63.

Hardin, Garrett. 1974. Living on a lifeboat. *BioScience* 24(10): 561–568.

Harris, Edmund. 2009. Neoliberal subjectivities or a politics of the possible? Reading for difference in alternative food networks. *Area* 41(1): 55–63.

Harris, Michael, and Bill Tayler. 2019. Don't let metrics undermine your business. *Harvard Business Review*, September–October.

Hart, Hornell. 1923. What is a social problem? *American Journal of Sociology* 29(3): 345–352.

Hassanein, Neva. 2003. Practicing food democracy: A pragmatic politics of transformation. *Journal of Rural Studies* 19(1): 77–86.

Heal, Geoffrey. 2012. Reflections: Defining and measuring sustainability. *Review of Environmental Economics and Policy* 6(1): 147–163.

Helliwell, John, Richard Layard, and Jeffrey Sachs. 2019. *World Happiness Report.* New York: Sustainable Development Solutions Network.

Herring, Horace, and Steve Sorrell, eds. 2009. *Energy Efficiency and Sustainable Consumption: The Rebound Effect*. New York: Palgrave Macmillan.

Hille, John. 1997. *The Concept of Environmental Space*. Copenhagen: European Environment Agency.

Höjer, Mattias, Anders Gullberg, and Ronny Pettersson. 2011. Backcasting images of the future city: Time and space for sustainable development in Stockholm. *Technological Forecasting and Social Change* 78: 819–834.

Holling, C. S. 2001. Understanding the complexity of economic, ecological, and social systems. *Ecosystems* 4(5): 390–405.

Howes, Michael, Liana Wortley, Ruth Potts, Aysin Dedekorkut-Howes, Silvia Serrao-Neumann, ... Patrick Nunn. 2017. Environmental sustainability: A case of policy implementation failure? *Sustainability* 9(2). https://www.mdpi.com/2071-1050/9/2/165/htm.

Huesemann, Michael. 2003. Recognizing the limits of environmental science and technology. *Environmental Science and Technology* 37(13): 259A–261A.

Huesemann, Michael, and Joyce Huesemann. 2011. *Techno-Fix: Why Technology Won't Save Us or the Environment*. Gabriola Island, BC: New Society.

ICDSI (Independent Commission on Disarmament and Security Issues). 1982. *Common Security: A Blueprint for Survival*. New York: Simon and Schuster.

ICIDI (Independent Commission on International Development Issues). 1980. *North–South: A Programme for Survival*. London: Pan Books.

IUCN (International Union for the Conservation of Nature). 1980. *World Conservation Strategy: Living Resource Conservation for Sustainable Development*. Gland, Switzerland: IUCN.

Jackson, Tim. 2017. *Prosperity without Growth: Foundations for the Economy of Tomorrow*, 2nd ed. New York: Routledge.

Jacobs, Meg. 2016. *Panic at the Pump: The Energy Crisis and the Transformation of American Politics in the 1970s*. New York: Hill and Wang.

Jamieson, Dale. 1998. Sustainability and beyond. *Ecological Economics* 24(2–3): 183–192.

Jevons, William Stanley. 1865. *The Coal Question: An Inquiring Concerning the Progress of the Nation, and the Probable Exhaustion of Our Coal Mines*. London: Macmillan and Company.

Johnson, Paul, Mark Everard, David Santillo, and Karl-Henrik Robért. 2007. Reclaiming the definition of sustainability. *Environmental Science and Pollution Research* 14(1): 60–66.

Jones, David. 2017. Restorative, heterotopic spacing for campus sustainability. *Environment and Planning D: Society and Space* 35(4): 752–771.

Kahn, Brian. 2015. Sea level could rise at least 6 meters. *Scientific American*, 9 July.

Kallis, Giorgos, Michael Kalush, Hugh O'Flynn, Jack Rossiter, and Nicholas Ashford. 2013. "Friday off": Reducing working hours in Europe. *Sustainability* 5(4): 1545–1567.

Kanger, Laur and Johan Schot. 2019. Deep Transitions: Theorizing the long-term patterns of socio-technical change. *Environmental Innovation and Societal Transitions* 32: 7–21.

Karvonen, Andrew, and Ralf Brand. 2007. Technical expertise, sustainability, and the politics of specialized knowledge. *Sustainability: Science, Practice, and Policy* 3(1): 21–31.

Kates, Robert, William Clark, Robert Corell, J. Michael Hall, Carlo Jaeger, … and Uno Svedin. 2001. Environment and development: Sustainability science. *Science* 292(5517): 641–642.

Kaufman, Alexander. 2018. What's the "Green New Deal"? The surprising origins behind a progressive rallying cry. *Grist*, 30 June.

Kaufman, Frederik. 2009. The end of sustainability. *International Journal of Sustainable Society* 1(4): 383–390.

Kennedy, Emily, Daphne Fecheyr-Lippens, Bor-Kai Hsiung, Peter Niewiarowski, and Matthew Kolodziej. 2015. Biomimicry: A path to sustainable innovation. *Design Issues* 31(3): 66–73.

Keynes, John Maynard. 1963 [1930]. *Essays in Persuasion*. New York: Harcourt, Brace and Company.

Kirk, Andrew. 2007. *Counterculture Green: The Whole Earth Catalog and American Environmentalism*. Lawrence, KS: University Press of Kansas.

Kitchin, Rob. 2014. The real-time city? Big data and smart urbanism. *GeoJournal* 79: 1–14.

Kondō, Marie. 2014. *The Life-Changing Magic of Tidying Up: The Japanese Art of Decluttering and Organizing*. New York: Ten Speed Press.

Kondratiev, Nikolai. 2014 [1935]. *The Long Waves of Economic Life*. Eastford, CT: Martino Fine Books.

Korten, David. 2010. *Agenda for a New Economy: From Phantom Wealth to Real Wealth*. San Francisco, CA: Berrett-Koehler Publishers.

Kurutz, Steven. 2009. Trashing the fridge. *New York Times*, February 5.

Larson, Brendon. 2014. *Metaphors for Environmental Sustainability: Redefining Our Relationship with Nature*. New Haven, CT: Yale University Press.

Laurent, Clint. 2013. *Tomorrow's World: A Look at the Demographic and Socioeconomic Structure of the World in 2032*. New York: Wiley.

Leaman, Adrian, and Bill Bordass. 2007. Are users more tolerant of "green" buildings? *Building Research and Information* 35(6): 662–673.

Lebreton, Laurent, Boyan Slat, Francesco Ferrari, Bruno Sainte-Rose, Jennifer Aitken, … Júlia Reisser. 2018. Evidence that the Great Pacific Garbage Patch is rapidly accumulating plastic. *Scientific Reports* 8(1), 4666. https://doi.org/10.1080/14036096.2020.1722218.

Lepenies, Philipp. 2019. Transforming by metrics that matter: Progress, participation, and the national initiatives of fixing well-being indicators. *Historical Social Research* 44(2): 288–312.

Letcher, Lisa. 2020. How the UK's first plastic-free town inspired the world. *CornwallLive*, 6 January.

Lettenmeier, Michael, Christa Liedtke, and Holger Rohn. 2014. Eight tons of material footprint: Suggestion for a resource cap for household consumption in Finland. *Resources* 3: 488–515.

Levidow, Les, and Helena Paul. 2011. Global agrofuel crops as contested sustainability, Part II: Eco-efficient techno-fixes? *Capitalism, Nature, Socialism* 22(2): 27–51.

Levitsky, Steven, and Daniel Ziblatt. 2018. *How Democracies Die: What History Reveals About Our Future*. New York: Viking.

Longo, Cristina, Avi Shankar, and Peter Nuttall. 2019. "It's not easy living a sustainable lifestyle": How greater knowledge leads to dilemmas, tensions and paralysis. *Journal of Business Ethics* 154(3): 759–779.

Lowenthal, David. 2016. Origins of Anthropocene awareness. *Anthropocene Review* 2(1): 1–12.

Magnusson, Margareta. 2018. *The Gentle Art of Swedish Death Cleaning: How to Free Yourself and Your Family from a Lifetime of Clutter*. New York: Scribner.

Malhi, Yadvinder. 2017. The concept of the Anthropocene. *Annual Review of Environment and Resources* 42: 77–104.

Mang, Pamela, and Bill Reed. 2012. Designing from place: A generative framework and methodology. *Building Research and Information* 40(1): 23–53.

Marchese, Dayton, Erin Reynolds, Matthew Bates, Heather Morgan, Sustain Clark, and Igor Linkov. 2018. Resilience and sustainability: Similarities and differences in environmental management applications. *Science of the Total Environment* 613–616: 1275–1283.

Martin, Chris, James Evans, and Andrew Karvonen. 2018. Smart and sustainable? Five tensions in the visions and practices of the smart-sustainable city in Europe and North America. *Technological Forecasting and Social Change* 133: 269–278.

McCormick, John. 1986. The origins of the World Conservation Strategy. *Environmental Review* 10(3): 177–187.

McDonough, William, and Michael Braungart. 2002. *Cradle to Cradle: Remaking the Way We Make Things*. New York: North Point Press.

McDonough, William, and Michael Braungart. 2013. *The Upcycle: Beyond Sustainability: Designing for Abundance*. New York: North Point Press.

McGinnis, Michael, ed. 1998. *Bioregionalism*. New York: Routledge.

McKibben, Bill. 2010. *Eaarth: Making a Life on a Tough New Planet*. New York: Times Books.

McMeekin, Andrew, Frank Geels, and Mike Hodson. 2019. Mapping the winds of whole system reconfiguration: Analysing low-carbon transformations across production, distribution and consumption in the UK electricity system (1990–2016). *Research Policy* 48(5): 1216–1231.

McNeill, J. R., and Peter Engelke. 2016. *The Great Acceleration: An Environmental History of the Anthropocene Since 1945*. Cambridge, MA: Harvard University Press.

Meadows, Donella. 2008. *Thinking in Systems: A Primer*. White River Junction, VT: Chelsea Green.

Meadows, Donella, Dennis Meadows, Jørgen Randers, and William Behrens. 1972. *The Limits to Growth*. New York: Universe Publishers.

Meir, Isaac, Yaakov Garb, Dixin Jiao, and Alex Cicelsky. 2009. Post-occupancy evaluation: An inevitable step toward sustainability. *Advances in Building Energy Research* 3(1): 189–220.

Mera, Roberto, Neil Massey, David Rupp, Philip Mote, Myles Allen, and Peter Frumhoff. 2015. Climate change, climate justice and the application of probabilistic event attribution to summer heat extremes in the California Central Valley. *Climatic Change* 133(3): 427–438.

Milestad, Rebecka, Åsa Svenfelt, and Karl Dreborg. 2014. Developing integrated explorative and normative scenarios: The case of future land use in climate-neutral Sweden. *Futures* 50: 59–71.

Millard, Jeremy, Marie Sorivelle, Sarah Deljanin, Elisabeth Unterfrauner, and Christian Voigt. 2018. Is the maker movement contributing to sustainability? *Sustainability* 10. https: //www.mdpi.com/2071-1050/10/7/2212/htm.

Mitcham, Carl. 1995. The concept of sustainable development: Its origin and ambivalence. *Technology in Society* 17(3): 311–326.

Mokyr, Joel. 1990. *The Lever of Riches: Technological Creativity and Economic Progress*. New York: Oxford University Press.

Mori, Koichiro, and Aris Christodoulou. 2012. Review of sustainability indices and indicators: Towards a new City Sustainability Index. *Environmental Impact Assessment Review* 32(1): 94–106.

Morozov, Evgeny. 2014. *To Save Everything, Click Here: The Folly of Technological Solutionism*. New York: Public Affairs.

Navarro, Vincente. 1984. A critique of the ideological and political positions of the Willy Brandt Report and the WHO Alma Ata Declaration. *Social Science and Medicine* 18(6): 467–474.

Nelson, Richard. 1993. *National Innovation Systems: A Comparative Analysis*. New York: Oxford University Press.

New Economics Foundation. 2016. *Happy Planet Index 2016: A Global Index of Sustainable Wellbeing*. London: NEF.

Nicholas, Tom. 2018. *The Death of Expertise: The Campaign Against Established Knowledge and Why It Matters*. New York: Oxford University Press.

Nordhaus, Ted, and Michael Shellenberger. 2005. The death of environmentalism: Global warming politics in a post-environmental world. *Grist*, 14 January.

Nordhaus, Ted, and Michael Scellenberger. 2007. *Break Through: From the Death of Environmentalism to the Politics of Possibility*. New York: Houghton Mifflin.

Norgaard, Richard. 1994. *Development Betrayed: The End of Progress and a Coevolutionary Revisioning of the Future*. New York: Routledge.

Norgaard, Richard. 1995. Beyond materialism: A coevolutionary reinterpretation of the environmental crisis. *Review of Social Economy* 53(4): 475–492.

Nye, David, David Tyfield, and John Urry. 2014. The United States and alternative energies since 1980: Technological fix or regime change? *Theory, Culture and Society* 31(5): 103–125.

OECD (Organisation for Economic Co-operation and Development). 2011. *Fostering Innovation to Address Social Challenges: Workshop Proceedings*. Paris: OECD.

OECD (Organisation for Economic Co-operation and Development), 2016. *OECD Science, Technology and Innovation Outlook 2016*. Paris: OECD.

Orr, David. 2014. The Oberlin Project. *Solutions Journal* 5(1): 7–12.

Ostrom, Elinor. 2009. A general framework for analyzing sustainability of social-ecological systems. *Science* 325(5939): 419–422.

Owen, David. 2011. *The Conundrum: How Scientific Innovation, Increased Efficiency, and Good Intentions Can Make Our Energy and Climate Problems Worse*. New York: Riverhead Books.

Parris, Thomas, and Robert Kates. 2003. Characterizing a sustainability transition: Goals, targets, trends, and driving forces. *Proceedings of the National Academy of Sciences* 100(14): 8068–8073.

Perez, Carlota. 2002. *Technological Revolutions and Financial Capital: The Dynamics of Bubbles and Golden Ages*. Northampton, MA: Edward Elgar.

Pettifor, Ann. 2019. *The Case for the Green New Deal*. London: Verso.

Philipsen, Dirk. 2015. *The Little Big Number: How GDP Came to Rule the World and What to Do About It*. Princeton, NJ: Princeton University Press.

Phipps, Lauren. 2018. The naked truth about clothing rental. *GreenBiz*, November 23.

Piketty, Thomas, Emmanuel Saez, and Gabriel Zucman. 2018. Distributional national accounts: Methods and estimates for the United States. *Quarterly Journal of Economics* 133(2): 553–609.

Pilling David. 2018. *The Growth Delusion: Wealth, Poverty, and the Well-Being of Nations*. New York: Crown Books.

Polanyi, Karl. 2001 [1944]. *The Great Transformation: The Political and Economic Origins of Our Time*. Boston: Beacon Press.

Polimeni, John, Kozo Mayumi, Mario Giampietro, and Blake Alcott. 2007. *The Jevons Paradox and the Myth of Resource Efficiency Improvements*. London: Earthscan.

Poole, Robert. 2008. *Earthrise: How Man First Saw the Earth*. New Haven, CT: Yale University Press.

Porter, Michael, and Claas van der Linde. 1995. Green and competitive: Ending the stalemate. *Harvard Business Review*, September–October.

Pullinger, Martin. 2014. Working time reduction policy in a sustainable economy: Criteria and options for its design. *Ecological Economics* 103: 11–19.

Raskin, Paul. 2011. Imagine all the people: Advancing a global citizens movement. *Kosmos Journal* (Spring/Summer): 4–6.

Raskin, Paul. 2016. *Journey to Earthland: The Great Transition to Planetary Civilization*. Boston, MA: Tellus Institute.

Raskin, Paul, Tariq Banuri, Gilberto Gallopín, Pablo Gutman, Al Hammond, … Rob Swart. 2002. *Great Transition: The Promise and Lure of the Times Ahead*. Boston, MA: Stockholm Environment Institute.

Raworth, Kate. 2017. *Doughnut Economics: 7 Ways to Think Like a 21st Century Economist*. White River Junction, VT: Chelsea Green.

Redclift, Michael. 1987. *Sustainable Development: Exploring the Contradictions*. London: Methuen.

Redclift, Michael. 1991. The multiple dimensions of sustainable development. *Geography* 76(1): 36–42.

Rees, William. 2009. The ecological crisis and self-delusion: Implications for the building sector. *Building Research and Information* 37(3): 300–311.

Rees, William, and Mathis Wackernagel. 1996. *Our Ecological Footprint: Reducing Human Impact on the Earth*. Gabriola Island, BC: New Society Press.

Rhodes, Christopher. 2015. Permaculture: regenerative – not merely sustainable. *Science Progress* 98(4): 403–412.

Rifkin, Jeremy. 2019. *The Green New Deal: Why the Fossil Fuel Civilization Will Collapse by 2028, and the Bold Economic Plan to Save Life on Earth*. New York: St. Martin's Press.

Rinkinen, Jenny, Elizabeth Shove, and Jacopo Torriti, eds. 2019. *Energy Fables: Challenging Ideas in the Energy Sector*. London: Earthscan.

Rittel, Horst, and Melvin Webber. 1973. Dilemmas in a general theory of planning. *Policy Sciences* 4: 155–169.

Robbins, Jim. 2001. Engineers ask nature for design advice. *New York Times*, December 11.

Robinson, John. 1982. Energy backcasting: A proposed method of policy analysis. *Energy Policy* 10(4): 337–345.

Robinson, John. 1988. Unlearning and backcasting: Rethinking some of the questions we ask about the future. *Technological Forecasting and Social Change* 33(4): 325–338.

Robinson, John, and Raymond Cole. 2015. Theoretical underpinnings of regenerative sustainability. *Building Research and Information* 43(2): 133–143.

Robinson, Nicholas. 2012. Beyond sustainability: Environmental management for the Anthropocene Epoch. *Journal of Public Affairs* 12(3): 181–194.

Rockström, Johan, Will Steffen, Kevin Noone, Åsa Persson, F. Stuart Chapin, … Jonathan Foley. 2009. Planetary boundaries: Exploring the safe operating space for humanity. *Ecology and Society* 14(2).

Rodrik. Dani. 2016. Premature deindustrialization. *Journal of Economic Growth* 21(1): 1–33.

Rogelj, Joeri, Michel den Elzen, Niklas Höhne, Taryn Fransen, Hanna Fekete, … Malte Meinshuausen. 2016. Paris Agreement climate proposals need a boost to keep warming well below 2°C. *Nature* 534(7609): 631–639.

Rohracher, Harald, and Philipp Späth. 2014. The interplay of urban energy policy and socio-technical transitions: The eco-cities of Graz and Freiburg in retrospect. *Urban Studies* 51(7): 1415–1431.

Rome, Adam. 2014. *The Genius of Earth Day: How a 1970 Teach-In Unexpectedly Made the First Green Generation*. New York: Hill and Wang.

Rosenberg Daneri, Daniel, Gregory Trencher, and John Petersen. 2015. Students as change agents in a town-side sustainability transformation: The Oberlin Project at Oberlin College. *Current Opinion in Environmental Sustainability* 16: 14–21.

Rostow, Walt. 1960. *The Stages of Economic Growth: A Non-Communist Manifesto*. New York: Cambridge University Press.

Sachs, Jeffrey. 2012. From millennium development goals to sustainable development goals. *The Lancet* 379 (9832): 2206–2211.

Sale, Kirkpatrick. 1985. *Dwellers in the Land: The Bioregional Vision*. San Francisco, CA: Sierra Club.

Samuelson, Pamela. 2016. Freedom to tinker. *Theoretical Inquiries in Law* 17(2): 563–600.

Sandin, Gustav, and Greg Peters. 2018. Environmental impact of textile reuse and recycling: A review. *Journal of Cleaner Production* 184: 353–365.

Schleper, Simone. 2017. Conservation compromises: The MAB and the legacy of the International Biological Program, 1964–1974. *Journal of the History of Biology* 59(1): 133–167.

Schor, Juliet. 2010. *Plenitude: The New Economics of True Wealth*. New York: Penguin.

Schot, Johan and Laur Kanger. 2018. Deep transitions: Emergence, acceleration, stabilization and directionality. *Research Policy* 47: 1045–1059.

Schumpeter, Joseph. 1961. *The Theory of Economic Development: An Inquiry into Profits, Capital, Credit, Interest, and the Business Cycle*, trans. Redvers Opie. New York: Oxford University Press.

Schwab, Klaus. 2016a. *The Fourth Industrial Revolution*. Geneva: World Economic Forum.

Schwab, Klaus. 2016b. The fourth industrial revolution: What it means, how to respond. *World Economic Forum*, January 14. https://www.weforum.org/agenda/2016/01/the-fourth-industrial-revolution-what-it-means-and-how-to-respond/.

Schwartz, Peter. 1991. *The Art of the Long View: Planning for the Future in an Uncertain World*. New York: Doubleday.

Sconfienza, Umberto. 2019. The post-sustainability trilemma. *Journal of Environmental Policy and Planning* 21(6): 769–784.

Seefried, Elke. 2015. Rethinking progress: On the origin of the modern sustainability discourse, 1970–2000. *Journal of Modern European History* 13(3): 377–400.

Segal, Howard. 2017. Practical utopias: America as techno-fix nation. *Utopian Studies* 28(2): 231–246.

Selden, Tom, and Daqing Song. 1994. Environmental quality and development: Is there a Kuznets Curve for air pollution emissions? *Journal of Environmental Economics and Management* 27(2): 147–162.

Sen, Amartya. 1999. *Development as Freedom*. New York: Oxford University Press.

Sharzer, Greg. 2012. *No Local: Why Small-Scale Alternatives Won't Change the World*. Washington, DC: Zero Books.

Shove, Elizabeth. 2018. What is wrong with energy efficiency? *Building Research and Information* 46(7): 779–789.

Simms, Andrew. 2009. A green New Deal: Poverty reduction and economic stability in a carbon-constrained world, pp. 208–218 in Felix Dodds, Andrew Higham, and Richard Sherman, eds., *Climate Change and Energy Insecurity: The Challenge for Peace, Security and Development*. New York: Routledge.

Solarz, Marcin. 2012. North–South, commemorating the first Brandt Report: Searching for the contemporary spatial picture of the global rift. *Third World Quarterly* 33(3): 559–569.

Spaargaren, Gert, and Arthur Mol. 1992. Sociology, environment, and modernity: Ecological modernization as a theory of social change. *Society and Natural Resources* 5(4): 323–344.

Speth, James. 2008. *The Bridge at the Edge of the World: Capitalism, the Environment, and Crossing from Crisis to Sustainability*. New Haven, CT: Yale University Press.

Steffen, Will, Paul Crutzen, and J. R. McNeill. 2007. The Anthropocene: Are humans now overwhelming the great forces of nature? *Ambio* 236(8): 614–621.

Steffen, Will, Wendy Broadgate, Lisa Deutsch, Owen Gaffney, and Cornelia Ludwig. 2015. The trajectory of the Anthropocene: The Great Acceleration. *The Anthropocene Review* 2(1): 81–98.

Stiglitz, Joseph, Amartya Sen, and Jean-Paul Fitoussi. 2010. *Mismeasuring Our Lives: Why GDP Doesn't Add Up*. New York: New Press.

Swilling, Mark, and Maarten Hajer. 2017. Governance of urban transitions: Towards sustainable resource efficient urban infrastructures. *Environmental Research Letters* 12(12), 125007. https://doi.org/10.1088/1748-9326/aa7d3a.

Tatzel, Miriam, ed. 2013. *Consumption and Well-being in the Material World*. New York: Springer.

Thompson, Jennifer. 2017. Surviving the 1970s: The case of Friends of the Earth. *Environmental History* 22(2): 235–256.

Toulmin, Stephen. 1992. *Cosmopolis: The Hidden Agenda of Modernity*. Chicago, IL: University of Chicago Press.

Trencher, Gregory, and Andrew Karvonen. 2019. Stretching "smart": Advancing health and well-being through the smart city agenda. *Local Environment* 24(7): 610–627.

Turner, Fred. 2008. *From Counterculture to Cyberculture: Stewart Brand, the Whole Earth Network, and the Rise of Digital Utopianism*. Chicago, IL: University of Chicago Press.

UNDESA (United Nations Department of Economic and Social Affairs). 2019. *SDG Progress Reports 2019: Are We on Track to Achieve the Global Goals?* New York: UNDESA.

UNDP (United Nations Development Program). 2018. *Human Development Indices and Indicators: 2018 Statistical Update*. New York: UNDP.

United Nations. 2012. *The Future We Want: Outcome Document of the*

United Nations Conference on Sustainable Development. New York: United Nations.

Usborne, Simon. 2018. How Penzance became Britain's first ever plastic-free town. *Guardian*, July 18.

Van der Voorn, Tom, Claudia Pahl-Wostl, and Jaco Quist. 2012. Combining backcasting and adaptive management for climate adaption in coastal regions: a methodology and a South African case study. *Futures* 44(4): 346–364.

Vermeulen, Sonja, Bruce Campbell, and John Ingram. 2012. Climate change and food systems. *Annual Review of Environment and Resources* 27: 195–222.

Vogelaar, Alison, Brack Hale, and Alexandra Peat. 2018. *The Discourses of Environmental Collapse: Imagining the End.* New York: Routledge.

Walker, Brian, C. S. Holling, Stephen Carpenter, and Ann Kinzig. 2004. Resilience, adaptability and transformability in socio-ecological systems. *Ecology and Society* 9(2), Article 5. https://www.ecologyandsociety.org/vol9/iss2/art5/.

Weber, Christopher, and H. Scott Matthews. 2008. Food-miles and the relative climate impacts of food choices in the United States. *Environmental Science and Technology* 42(10): 3508–3513.

Weyler, Rex. 2004. *Greenpeace: How a Group of Ecologists, Journalists, and Visionaries Changed the World.* Emmaus, PA: Rodale Press.

Whitmee, Sarah, Andy Haines, Chris Beyrer, Frederick Boltz, Anthony Capon, … Derek Yach. 2015. Safeguarding human health in the Anthropocene epoch: Report of the Rockefeller Foundation-Lancet Commission on planetary health. *The Lancet* 386(10007): 1973–2028.

Wiedmann, Thomas, Heinz Schandl, Manfred Lenzen, Daniel Moran, Sangwon Suh, … Keiichiro Kanemoto. 2015. The material footprint of nations. *Proceedings of the National Academy of Sciences* 112(20): 6271–6276.

Worster, Donald. 1993. *The Wealth of Nature: Environmental History and the Ecological Imagination.* New York: Oxford University Press.

Yourgrau, Barry. 2015. The origin story of Marie Kondo's decluttering empire. *The New Yorker*, 8 December.

Zalasiewicz, Jan, Colin Waters, Juliana Ivar do Sul, Patricia Corcoran, Anthony Barnosky, … Yasmin Yonan. 2016. The geological cycle of plastics and their use as a stratigraphic indicator of the Anthropocene. *Anthropocene* 13: 4–17.

Zelov, Chris, and Phil Cousineau. 1997. *Design Outlaws on the Ecological Frontier.* Philadelphia, PA: Knossus Publishing.

Zolli, Andrew, and Ann Marie Healy. 2012. *Resilience: Why Things Bounce Back.* New York: Free Press.

Zolli, Andrew. 2012. Learning to bounce back. *New York Times*, November 2.

Index